COOK good FOOD

FROM THE EDITORS OF
WILLIAMS-SONOMA

PHOTOGRAPHS BY EVA KOLENKO

weldon**owen**

CONTENTS

MAKE *good* FOOD TONIGHT

If you're ready to take your cooking skills up a notch, and move beyond mixing canned tomato sauce with boiled pasta or relying on frozen meals for dinner, we're here to help. With this book as your guide, you'll become more confident in the kitchen and up your cooking game, while having fun along the way.

Within these pages are straightforward lessons covering six basic cooking techniques: sautéing, stir-frying, frying, braising, simmering & poaching, and steaming, all of which can be done with just a basic set of pots and pans—no special equipment needed. Each easy-to understand lesson presents the key tools you'll need, the secrets of success for that method, and answers to common cooking questions.

If there's one takeaway from reading this book, it's simply that you'll learn to cook good food.

We've also included step-by-step instructions with full-color photos, so there's no mystery involved in the process. Don't worry about having fancy knife skills; if you know how to chop and mince (which is another way to say finely chop), you're good to go.

Each lesson is followed by ten recipes for fresh and flavorful food that's fit for everyday noshing or even hosting a party for friends. And you'll enjoy cooking these dishes as much as eating them. Use this book as your personal kitchen handbook, a go-to collection of reliable recipes, or both—it's up to you. But if there's one takeaway from this book, it's simply that you'll learn to cook good food.

SAUTÉ

ALL ABOUT
SAUTÉING

Sautéing comes from the French word for "jump," and it's a way to cook small pieces of food by turning them quickly in a hot pan. Sautéing can also be used for larger pieces of food, like pork chops, that are turned only once to encourage browning. You often hear the word "pan-frying" used synonymously with sautéing, but pan-frying typically calls for a bit more fat than the thin film you need when sautéing.

To sauté means to quickly cook food in a small amount of oil over high heat. Foods best suited to sautéing are generally lean, tender, and cut into small pieces.

For the best results, choose a sauté pan that seems heavy for its size, is sturdy, and is made of a quality metal so that it will heat evenly. Choose a neutral-flavored cooking oil for sautéing, one that can withstand the medium-high to high cooking temperatures needed to achieve the deep, golden brown color that sautéing imparts to food. Butter can also be used for quick sautéing, but be sure to watch it closely as it browns easily.

Professional chefs use a quick flick of the wrist to toss sautéed ingredients in the air in a flamboyant fashion, but for most home cooks, you'll want to use tongs or a wooden spoon or spatula to turn the food.

WHAT DOES "SMOKE POINT" MEAN?

Smoke point is the temperature at which oil begins to break down and emit smoke. Some types of oil have a higher smoke point than others, and so are preferred for cooking techniques that employ high heat, such as sautéing, stir-frying, and frying. Oils with high smoke points include canola oil, grapeseed oil, peanut oil, and refined olive oil.

STRAIGHT-SIDED SAUTÉ PAN
OR SLOPE-SIDED FRYING PAN

SECRETS TO SUCCESS

PAT FOODS DRY
Soak up the moisture on foods' surface with paper towels before sautéing. A dry surface will encourage browning.

DO NOT CROWD
Crowding food in the pan will create steam and inhibit browning. Use a pan that is large enough to fit the ingredients comfortably in a single layer, or cook the food in batches.

RESIST THE URGE TO MOVE THE FOOD
When cooking meat or poultry, don't turn it until it is browned on the underside. If the food seems stuck to the pan, it usually means the food is not ready to be flipped.

COOK THE SIDE YOU PRESENT FIRST
When cooking meat, poultry, or fish, the first side cooked will often look better than the second side. Be sure to put the prettiest side facedown in the pan when you begin to sauté.

PREHEAT THE PAN
Once the pan is hot, add the oil and heat it for a few seconds before adding the food. To test the heat level, hold your hand over the pan; you should feel the heat rising.

SET OF RESTAURANT-STYLE TONGS

WOODEN SPOON OR SPATULA

OIL WITH A HIGH SMOKE POINT

NONSTICK VS. UNCOATED SAUTÉ PANS

Nonstick pans are coated with a substance that helps foods release easily and clean up quickly. While nonstick pots and pans are convenient, if you are browning meats or making a pan sauce, you will get better results and fuller flavor from uncoated pans.

MEDIUM-HIGH TO HIGH HEAT

HOW TO
SAUTÉ

1

HEAT THE PAN
You'll feel the heat radiating up when it's hot enough to start cooking.

2

SWIRL IN THE OIL
When you see the surface of the oil shimmer, you're good to go.

3

ADD THE FOOD
Leave it undisturbed for a few seconds to encourage caramelization.

4

STIR & TOSS
When you see browning, stir and toss with a wooden spoon or tongs. Repeat every few seconds to encourage even cooking.

5
DEGLAZE
If you're making a pan sauce, add broth or wine and scrape up the delicious browned bits that stick to the bottom of the pan.

6
REDUCE & FINISH
To finish a pan sauce, vigorously simmer the liquid until it is a sauce consistency. Stir in butter or mustard to thicken the pan sauce.

MUSHROOM & GOAT CHEESE BRUSCHETTA

MAKES 8 BRUSCHETTA

These topped toasts are awesome for parties: They make great
finger food and look deceptively fancy. All it really takes is a few slices
of toasted bread, a slathering of goat cheese, and a topping of
sautéed mushrooms—seriously easy and seriously impressive.

1 Warm a sauté pan over medium-high heat. Add the butter and oil
and warm until the butter melts. Add the mushrooms and ¼ teaspoon
salt and sauté, stirring often, until the mushrooms begin to release
their juices, 2–3 minutes.

2 Toast the bread, then arrange on a platter. Spread each piece with
a thin layer of goat cheese.

3 Top the toasts with the mushrooms, dividing evenly, sprinkle with
chives, and season lightly with salt and pepper. Serve right away.

{ LIFE OF THE PARTY: BRUSCHETTA
With good-quality bread as your base, you can top these
toasts with virtually anything, and pass them as finger food.
A sprinkling of fresh herbs, high-quality olive oil, or freshly
ground pepper goes a long way toward presentation.

**Unsalted butter,
2 teaspoons**

Olive oil, 1 tablespoon

**Assorted mushrooms
such as cremini, shiitake,
oyster, or chanterelle,
½ lb (250 g), stemmed,
and halved or quartered**

**Kosher salt and freshly
ground pepper**

**Coarse country bread,
8 slices**

**Soft fresh goat cheese,
4 oz (125 g)**

Fresh chives, chopped

CHICKEN MEATBALLS
WITH GINGER & LEMONGRASS

MAKES 3-4 SERVINGS

Who said meatballs only belong in sauces and pastas? Here ground chicken is mixed with fresh and tangy Asian flavors and rolled into bite-sized balls. Wrap them up in supercrunchy and fresh lettuce leaves for a bright and inspired meal.

1 Preheat the oven to 350°F (180°C). Lightly oil a baking sheet.

2 In a bowl, combine the chicken, panko, soy sauce, fish sauce, lemongrass, cornstarch, cilantro, ginger, and garlic. Season with salt and pepper and mix well. Roll into 1-inch (2.5-cm) balls.

3 Warm a large sauté pan or frying pan over medium heat. Add the ¼ cup (2 fl oz/60 ml) oil and heat until it appears to shimmer. Add the meatballs and sauté, turning the meatballs to brown evenly on all sides, about 5 minutes total. Drain on paper towels. Transfer the meatballs to the prepared baking sheet and bake until cooked through, 3–5 minutes.

4 Arrange the lettuce, green onions, and limes on a platter. Serve the meatballs in a bowl on the side. Instruct guests to place a meatball in a lettuce leaf, top with green onions, squeeze with lime juice, fold, and eat.

{ INGREDIENT DEMYSTIFIED: LEMONGRASS
Lemongrass is an herblike stalk used in Southeast Asian cuisine. It looks similar to a green onion. Only the pale bottom part of the stalk is used in cooking. Crush the stalk with the flat side of a chef's knife before finely mincing to make it easier to work with and release the flavor.

Grapeseed oil, ¼ cup (2 fl oz/60 ml), plus more for oiling the baking sheet

Ground chicken, 1 lb (500 g)

Panko bread crumbs, 2 tablespoons

Soy sauce, 1 tablespoon

Asian fish sauce, 1 tablespoon

Lemongrass, white part only, 1 tablespoon minced

Cornstarch, 1 tablespoon

Fresh cilantro, 1 tablespoon chopped

Fresh ginger, 1½ teaspoons minced

Garlic, 1 clove, minced

Kosher salt and freshly ground pepper

Small lettuce leaves, 14

Green onions, 4, thinly sliced

Limes, 2, cut into wedges

PORK CHOPS
WITH MUSTARD & CAPER PAN SAUCE

MAKES 4 SERVINGS

For the best flavor and texture, seek out pork from a local rancher, who might hawk their wares at a farmers' market or upscale food market. The amazing pan sauce calls for just 5 ingredients and uses the luscious browned bits from sautéing the chops.

1 Remove the pork chops from the refrigerator and let stand for 30 minutes. Pat the chops dry with paper towels and season both sides generously with salt and pepper. Preheat the oven to 200°F (95°C) and place a platter in the oven to warm.

2 Warm a large sauté pan or frying pan over high heat and add half of the oil. When the oil appears to shimmer, reduce the heat to medium-high, add 2 chops, and sear without moving them for 2½ minutes. Turn and cook until the chops are golden and firm to the touch, but still have a little give, about 2½ minutes more. If you like, insert an instant-read thermometer horizontally into a chop, away from the bone; it should register 140°F (60°C) for medium-rare. Transfer the chops to the warm platter and keep warm in the oven. Repeat with the remaining oil and the remaining chops.

3 Pour any oil from the pan. Reduce the heat to medium and add the capers to the pan. Cook for 1 minute. Add the wine, bring to a simmer, and cook until reduced by about half, about 2 minutes. Stir in the cream, vinegar, and ¼ teaspoon salt and season with pepper. Simmer the sauce until lightly thickened, about 30 seconds. Remove from the heat and whisk in the mustard. Taste and adjust the seasoning.

4 Pour some of the sauce over the chops on the platter. Serve right away, passing the remaining sauce at the table.

Center-cut pork loin chops,
4, each about 7 oz (220 g)
and ¾ inch (2 cm) thick

Kosher salt and freshly
ground pepper

Olive oil, 1½ tablespoons

Capers, ⅓ cup
(2½ oz/75 g)

Dry white wine, 1¼ cups
(10 fl oz/310 ml)

Heavy cream, ⅓ cup
(3 fl oz/80 ml)

White wine vinegar,
¼ teaspoon

Whole-grain mustard,
2 tablespoons

CRAB CAKES
WITH SRIRACHA MAYO

MAKES 6 CRAB CAKES

When you buy precooked and packaged crabmeat from your local fishmonger, making crab cakes is really easy. This recipe can be doubled to feed a crowd, or you can make 12 smaller cakes for appetizers. Sriracha mayo is both creamy and spicy, and it's the perfect complement to lightly sautéed shellfish of any kind.

1 To make the Sriracha mayo, in a bowl, mix together the mayonnaise, Sriracha, and lemon juice to taste. Season with salt and pepper. Cover and refrigerate until ready to serve.

2 In a bowl, combine the crabmeat, bread crumbs, mayonnaise, and chives, and mix gently until the ingredients are evenly distributed, being careful not to break up the chunks of crabmeat. Season to taste with salt and pepper.

3 Shape the crab mixture into 6 equal-sized cakes and place them on a plate. Cover and refrigerate for at least 10 minutes or up to overnight to allow the bread crumbs to absorb some of the juices.

4 Warm a sauté pan or frying pan over medium-high heat and add the butter and oil. When the butter has melted, add the crab cakes and cook until golden on the undersides, 3–4 minutes. Flip the cakes over and cook on the second sides until golden, 3–4 minutes longer, reducing the heat if needed to avoiding overcooking the exterior.

5 Serve the crab cakes right away with the lemon wedges for squeezing and the Sriracha mayo on the side for dipping.

{ **PREP WORK: HOMEMADE BREAD CRUMBS**
Lay a few slices of your favorite bread on the countertop to dry out overnight, or use stale bread. Tear the bread into large pieces and process in a blender or food processor to the texture you want.

FOR THE SRIRACHA MAYO
Good-quality mayonnaise, 1 cup (8 fl oz/250 ml)

Sriracha sauce, 1–2 tablespoons

Fresh lemon juice

Kosher salt and freshly ground pepper

FOR THE CRAB CAKES
Crabmeat, ½ lb (250 g), picked over for shell fragments and cartilage

Fresh white bread crumbs, 1 cup (2 oz/60 g)

Good-quality mayonnaise, ¼ cup (2 fl oz/60 ml)

Fresh chives, 1 tablespoon chopped

Kosher salt and freshly ground pepper

Unsalted butter, 1 tablespoon

Olive oil, 1 tablespoon

Lemon wedges, for serving

LEMON-BUTTER SHRIMP

MAKES 4 SERVINGS

Similar to a scampi dish, the shrimp here is lightly dusted in flour for a crisp coating and then tossed in a reduced wine, lemon, and butter sauce. Sop up the creamy sauce with warm crusty bread or mix the contents of the frying pan into a bowl of cooked spaghetti.

1 In a shallow bowl, stir together the flour, ½ teaspoon salt, and ¼ teaspoon pepper. Warm a large sauté pan or frying pan over medium-high heat and add the oil. Toss half of the shrimp in the flour mixture to coat evenly, shaking off the excess. Add the shrimp to the hot pan and cook, turning occasionally, until opaque throughout when pierced with the tip of a paring knife, about 3 minutes. Transfer to a plate and tent with aluminum foil to keep warm. Repeat with the remaining shrimp, adding more oil as needed.

2 Reduce the heat to medium-low. Add 2 tablespoons of the butter and the garlic to the pan and sauté until the garlic is softened and fragrant but not browned, about 2 minutes. Add the wine and the lemon zest and juice and bring to a boil over high heat. Cook until reduced by half, about 1 minute. Reduce the heat to very low. One tablespoon at a time, whisk in the remaining 10 tablespoons butter, letting each addition soften into a creamy emulsion before adding more.

3 Return the shrimp to the sauce and mix gently to coat well. Remove from the heat and season the sauce with salt and pepper. Transfer to a serving dish and sprinkle with the parsley. Serve right away, with the lemon wedges for squeezing.

All-purpose flour, ½ cup (2½ oz/75 g)

Kosher salt and freshly ground pepper

Olive oil, 2 tablespoons, plus more as needed

Jumbo shrimp, 1½ lb (750 g), peeled and deveined

Unsalted butter, 12 tablespoons (1½ sticks/6 oz/185 g)

Garlic, 3 cloves, minced

Dry white wine, ¼ cup (2 fl oz/60 ml)

Lemon zest, grated from 1 lemon

Fresh lemon juice, 2 tablespoons

Fresh flat-leaf parsley, 2 tablespoons finely chopped

Lemon wedges, for serving

SKILLET CHEESEBURGERS

MAKES 4 BURGERS

You don't need to fire up an outdoor grill to create a sublime burger—a really hot sauté pan does a great job, too. For the best flavor and texture, buy your ground beef from a butcher shop that grinds the meat on the premises; stay away from supermarket beef in a cellophane package.

1 In a bowl, combine the ground beef, garlic powder, and ½ teaspoon pepper. Using a fork, stir it together, keeping the mixture crumbly rather than compressed.

2 With a light hand, form 4 loosely packed patties, then gently flatten each patty to about ½ inch (12 mm) thick. Refrigerate the patties for 15 minutes.

3 Warm a large, heavy sauté pan or frying pan over high heat until it is very hot, 2–3 minutes. Reduce the heat to medium-high, brush the tops of the patties with oil, and season generously with salt. Place the patties in the pan, oiled side down, and cook, without moving them, for 3 minutes. Brush the tops of the patties with oil, season generously with salt, and turn and cook until an instant-read thermometer inserted into a burger registers 140° (60°C) for medium, 5–7 minutes more, or to your desired doneness. Add a slice of cheese to the top of each patty during the last 2 minutes of cooking and let it melt.

4 Arrange the patties in the buns. Set out the sliced onion and tomato, and the mayonnaise, ketchup, and mustard for topping the burgers. Serve right away.

{ **FAT IS FINE** For the best flavor and juicy texture, you want your ground beef to have about 20% fat. When making burgers, don't opt for the lean beef. It's time to splurge!

Ground beef chuck, 1½ lb (750 g)

Garlic powder, ½ teaspoon

Kosher salt and freshly ground pepper

Olive oil, for brushing

Cheddar cheese, 4 slices

Hamburger buns, preferably from a local bakery, split and toasted

Sliced red onion and sliced tomato, for serving

Mayonnaise, ketchup, or mustard, for serving

SPICY SAUTÉED KALE & CHICKPEAS

MAKES 4 SERVINGS

Covering the pan initially allows the kale to steam, infusing it with
the scent of garlic, and softening its rigid structure. This is a superhealthy
anytime meal that's composed of all pantry staples, besides the kale.
It makes a terrific vegetarian main or side dish.

1 Warm a large sauté pan or frying pan over medium-low heat. Add the garlic and oil and sauté, stirring often, until softened but not browned, about 7 minutes.

2 Put about half of the kale in the pan. Cover and let wilt for about 2 minutes, then uncover and add the rest of the kale. Using tongs, turn the kale to coat with the oil and garlic. Cover the pan and cook until the kale is tender, 15–20 minutes.

3 Uncover and stir in the chickpeas, pepper flakes, and 1 teaspoon salt. Raise the heat to medium and sauté until the chickpeas are heated through, about 5 minutes. Serve right away.

Garlic, 3 large cloves, very thinly sliced

Olive oil, ¼ cup (2 fl oz/60 ml)

Lacinato kale, 1 lb (500 g), tough stems removed, leaves coarsely chopped

Chickpeas, 1 can (14 oz/440 g) rinsed and drained

Red pepper flakes, pinch

Kosher salt

{ **PREP WORK: WASHING LEAFY GREENS**
Leafy greens can hide a lot of dirt in their crevices, so be sure to wash them well before using. Chop the greens first (remember to wash the cutting board after using). Then, fill a large bowl with cold water and immerse the greens in the water. Swish the greens around with your hands for a few seconds, then let them stand so that the dirt and grit falls to the bottom of the bowl. Scoop the greens from the bowl and discard the rinsing water. If the greens are very dirty, repeat the rinsing one or more times.

CHICKEN CUTLETS
WITH OLIVE-LEMON RELISH

MAKES 2 SERVINGS

This recipe yields a lot of relish, and that's a good thing, because you'll want extra for spreading on toast, mixing into pastas, and whisking into salad dressings. The salty and sour mixture makes a colorful and textural topping for golden-brown chicken cutlets. Serve this dish with a simple arugula salad on the side for a complete meal.

1 To make the relish, finely grate half of the zest from the lemon, then squeeze 1 tablespoon lemon juice. Turn on a food processor and drop the garlic through the feed tube to chop it. Stop the machine, add the olives, capers, parsley, pepper flakes, and lemon zest and juice, and pulse to chop the olives coarsely. With the machine running, slowly pour in the oil and process until the olives are finely chopped. Transfer to a bowl, cover, and let stand while you cook the chicken.

2 Using a flat meat pounder, pound each chicken breast half until flattened to an even thickness of about ½ inch (12 mm).

3 In a shallow dish, stir together the flour, ¼ teaspoon salt, and ¼ teaspoon black pepper. In a second shallow dish, whisk together the egg and 1½ tablespoons of the olive oil. In a third shallow dish, stir together the panko, oregano, and basil.

4 Dip 1 chicken breast in the flour mixture, coating it evenly and shaking off the excess. Then dip it in the egg mixture, coating evenly and allowing the excess to drip off. Finally, coat it evenly with the bread crumb mixture. Transfer to a clean plate. Repeat with the remaining chicken breast. Let stand for 5 minutes.

5 Warm a large sauté pan or frying pan over medium heat and add 2 tablespoons oil. Add the chicken breasts and cook, turning once and adjusting the heat as needed to prevent scorching, until golden brown, 3–4 minutes per side. Using a slotted spatula, transfer the chicken to a paper towel–lined plate to drain briefly. Transfer the chicken to a platter and serve right away, passing the relish at the table.

FOR THE RELISH
Lemon, 1

Garlic, 1 small clove

Pitted green olives, 1 cup (5 oz/155 g)

Capers, 1½ tablespoons

Fresh flat-leaf parsley, 1½ tablespoons chopped

Red pepper flakes, pinch

Extra-virgin olive oil, ¼ cup (2 fl oz/60 ml)

Skinless, boneless chicken breast halves, 2, about 6 oz (185 g) each

All-purpose flour, ¼ cup (1½ oz/45 g)

Kosher salt and freshly ground black pepper

Large egg, 1

Olive oil, 3½ tablespoons

Panko bread crumbs, ½ cup (1 oz/30 g)

Dried oregano, ½ tsp

Dried basil, ½ tsp

TURKEY SALTIMBOCCA

MAKES 4-6 SERVINGS

Saltimbocca, an ambitious-sounding dish, is actually quite simple.
Turkey cutlets are lightly sautéed until golden, then dressed in a pan sauce
of prosciutto, fresh sage, and reduced wine. The turkey can easily
be replaced by chicken breasts that have been pounded thin.

1 Preheat the oven to 350°F (180°C). Put the flour in a shallow bowl. Season the cutlets on both sides with salt and pepper, and then coat both sides with the flour and tap off the excess. Place on a plate.

2 Warm a large ovenproof sauté pan or frying pan over medium-high heat and add 1 tablespoon of the butter. When it begins to brown, add the oil and then add the cutlets. Cook, turning once, until golden, 3–4 minutes per side. Transfer the pan to the oven to finish cooking, about 5 minutes. Using tongs, transfer the cutlets to a warmed platter.

3 Place the pan over medium-high heat and add 1 tablespoon of the butter. When the butter begins to brown, add the prosciutto and sage and sauté until the prosciutto is puckered and golden, about 2 minutes. Add the wine, bring to a boil, stir, and boil for 1–2 minutes to reduce slightly. Remove from the heat and swirl in the remaining 2 tablespoons butter. Season to taste with salt and pepper. Spoon the sauce over the cutlets and serve right away.

All-purpose flour, ½ cup
(2½ oz/75 g)

Turkey cutlets, 6, each
about ¼ lb (125 g)
and ½ inch (12 mm) thick

Kosher salt and freshly
ground pepper

Unsalted butter,
4 tablespoons (2 oz/60 g)

Olive oil, 1 tablespoon

Thinly sliced prosciutto,
¼ lb (125 g), cut into
narrow strips

Fresh sage, 2 tablespoons
chopped

Dry white wine, ½ cup
(4 fl oz/125 ml)

{ PREP WORK: MAKING CUTLETS
If turkey cutlets aren't readily available at the store,
it's easy to make your own. Place a skinless, boneless
chicken or turkey breast between 2 sheets of waxed paper
or plastic wrap. Using a flat meat pounder or rolling pin,
pound the meat until it's ¼–½ inch (6–12 mm) thick.
Pounding is also a great stress reliever!

SEARED TOMATOES
WITH ARUGULA PESTO & FETA

MAKES 4 SERVINGS

You may not think to cook tomatoes whole, but this is a great recipe to keep
in mind during summer's tomato season. Here, multicolored cherry and pear tomatoes
are sautéed until just softened, so that they explode with fresh flavor when eaten.
This warm salad is delicious with some crusty bread from the bakery.

1 To make the pesto, preheat the oven to 375°F (190°C). Pour the
walnuts onto a rimmed baking sheet. Toast the nuts in the oven
until they turn a shade or two darker and are fragrant, 6–8 minutes.
Pour the nuts onto a plate to cool.

2 Finely grate the zest from the lemon (reserve the fruit for another
use). In the bowl of a food processor, combine the toasted walnuts,
lemon zest, and garlic and pulse just to combine. Add the basil and
arugula leaves and process until coarsely chopped. With the machine
running, slowly pour in the ¼ cup (2 fl oz/60 ml) oil. Continue to
process until the mixture is moist and well blended but still slightly
chunky. Transfer the pesto to a small bowl and taste and adjust the
seasonings with salt and pepper.

3 Warm a sauté pan or frying pan over medium-high heat, and add the
1 tablespoon oil. Add the tomatoes and a pinch of salt and sauté until
the tomatoes are warmed through and their skins are just beginning
to split, 3–4 minutes. Remove from the heat and stir in the pesto.

4 Transfer the tomatoes to a serving dish and crumble the cheese
over the top. Serve warm or at room temperature.

FOR THE ARUGULA PESTO
Walnuts, 3 tablespoons

Lemon zest, grated
from 1 lemon

Garlic, 1 clove,
roughly chopped

Fresh basil leaves,
from ¼ bunch

Baby arugula leaves, 1 cup
(1 oz/30 g) packed

Olive oil, ¼ cup
(2 fl oz/60 ml)

Kosher salt and freshly
ground pepper

Olive oil, 1 tablespoon

Multicolor cherry and pear
tomatoes, 1½ lb (750 g)

Feta cheese, 2 oz (60 g)

STIR-FRY

ALL ABOUT
STIR-FRYING

Stir-frying is a quick cooking method that comes from Chinese cooking traditions. It involves tossing and stirring small pieces of food in very a small amount of oil over very high heat. It is the ultimate one-pan cooking method, where chopped and sliced ingredients are cooked in batches, and then added back to the pan at the end for a complete dish. Often a boldly flavored sauce is added at the end to bring the dish together.

Stir-frying is essentially a high-heat, high-speed version of sautéing, where bite-sized ingredients are tossed quickly in smoking-hot oil.

A wok, a heavy metal pan with a rounded bottom and sloping sides, is the classic pan for stir-frying in China and other Asian countries, as its shape helps to quickly move the food around in the pan during cooking. You can also use a straight-sided sauté pan or Dutch oven for this cooking method. Like with sautéing, you'll need to choose an oil that has a high smoke point to withstand the high temperature needed for proper stir-frying.

Done efficiently, stir-frying is a two-handed cooking technique. You'll want to have two sturdy wooden or metal spatulas, or two wooden spoons, in a pinch, to help stir and toss the food over the high heat.

DO I NEED A WOK TO STIR-FRY?

A wok, with its high, sloping sides, is a great tool for stir-frying thanks to its large surface area and deep bowl that helps keep foods from escaping as you are tossing and stirring the ingredients over high heat. But if you don't have a wok in your pots-and-pans collection, a straight-sided sauté pan works well, too. You may need to chase down a few errant items if you toss a bit too vigorously!

SMALL & MEDIUM BOWLS FOR PREPPED INGREDIENTS

WOK OR LARGE STRAIGHT-SIDED SAUTÉ PAN

SECRETS TO SUCCESS

PREP FIRST Make sure you have all your ingredients sliced, measured, and within easy reach of the stove before you begin.

HEAT THE PAN Warm it for a few minutes before starting. You know it's ready when you feel pronounced heat rising when you hold your hand above it.

SWIRL AWAY Once the pan is hot, add the oil and quickly but carefully tilt and rotate the pan so that the oil is distributed over the surface. You are supposed to use the whole surface area of the pan when stir-frying, so be sure all parts are well coated.

TIMING IS EVERYTHING To ensure even cooking, add the slowest-cooking ingredients to the pan first, and end with the fastest cooking ingredients. Or, add individual ingredients to the pan in batches, and pour them onto a plate when they are done. Recombine the ingredients just before serving to heat them through.

2 WOODEN OR METAL SPATULAS OR SPECIALIZED WOK TOOLS

USE TWO HANDS The quick cooking pace and high heat that stir-frying demands means it's best to use two hands when cooking, tossing and stirring the ingredients rapidly and pushing them up the sides of the pan to expose them evenly to the heat.

OIL WITH A HIGH SMOKE POINT

DOS AND DON'TS: FATS & OILS FOR STIR-FRYING

DO use peanut, grapeseed, canola, or a similar oil that has a high smoke point.

DON'T use butter, olive oil, or dark sesame oil for stir-frying, as they cannot withstand high heat without burning.

MEDIUM-HIGH TO HIGH HEAT

HOW TO
STIR-FRY

1

ASSEMBLE YOUR STUFF
Since stir-frying goes so fast,
it's helpful to have everything ready
and near the stove before you start.

2

ADD THE FIRST INGREDIENT
Stir-fried recipes often call for adding
the ingredients in batches. After
swirling the oil into the hot pan,
add the first ingredient.

3

STIR & TOSS
Leave the food undisturbed for a
few seconds to encourage browning,
then grab your tools and stir and
toss vigorously with both hands.

4

REMOVE & REPEAT

Transfer the first ingredient
to a plate or bowl, then add
the next set of ingredients
to the pan and repeat
the stirring and tossing.

5

RE-COMBINE & FINISH

Add all the ingredients back
to the pan. Add the finishing
sauce, if using, and stir to
heat through and thicken.

SALT & PEPPER SHRIMP

MAKES 6–8 SERVINGS

This dish is as easy as it gets—just 6 ingredients, 4 steps, and 3 minutes cooking time results in crispy shrimp that burst with flavor. Don't be scared of the shrimp heads, they can easily be popped off by hand or chopped off after cooking.

1 Put the peppercorns in a spice grinder (or a clean coffee grinder reserved only for grinding spices) and pulse several times until the peppercorns are finely crushed.

2 In a bowl, combine the shrimp, half of the crushed peppercorns, and 1 teaspoon salt and toss together well. Set aside.

3 Warm a wok or a large frying pan over medium-high heat, then swirl in the oil. Add the garlic, remaining peppercorns, and 1 teaspoon salt and stir-fry for 1 minute. Add the shrimp and stir-fry until opaque throughout, 3–4 minutes; the shrimp cooks really fast—be careful not to overcook them.

4 Serve right away with the lemon wedges for squeezing. Place a small bowl or dish on the table for discarded shells. And don't forget to put out plenty of napkins!

Multicolored peppercorns,
1 teaspoon

Large shrimp in the shell,
2 lb (1 kg), heads on,
if available

Sea salt

Grapeseed oil, 2 tablespoons

Garlic, 4 cloves, minced

Lemon wedges, for serving

{ **TIPS ON BUYING SHRIMP** To be sure you are buying the best possible seafood, it's a good idea to buy from a local fish market that has high turnover of their products. Heads-on shrimp have the best flavor, but can be hard to find. Choose firm, sweet-smelling, in-the-shell shrimp. Pass over shrimp with an "off" odor or a gritty feel. Fresh, raw shrimp should be used within 24 hours of purchase. If good-looking fresh shrimp are not available near you, opt for frozen shrimp, which should be fully thawed before cooking.

MU SHU PORK

MAKES 4 SERVINGS

Traditional Mandarin pancakes can be hard to find, but can sometimes
be located in Asian food stores. Easier-to-find soft corn tortillas (usually
a blend of corn and wheat) will work just as well in this easy homemade riff
on Chinese takeout. If you like, substitute chicken breast for the pork.

1 Cut the pork across the grain into thin strips. In a bowl, mix the pork with 1 tablespoon of the soy sauce, the sherry, cornstarch, and 1 teaspoon of the ginger. In a small bowl, stir together the hoisin sauce, 1 tablespoon of the soy sauce, 1 teaspoon of the sesame oil, and 1 tablespoon of the water. Set aside.

2 Warm a wok or a large frying pan over medium-high heat, then swirl in 1 tablespoon of the grapeseed oil. Beat the eggs with a pinch of salt, add them to the pan, and let stand until puffy, about 30 seconds. Stir until the eggs are just set, about 30 seconds; transfer to a plate.

3 Return the pan to medium-high heat and add 1 tablespoon of the grapeseed oil. Add the pork mixture and stir-fry until cooked through, about 3 minutes; add to the plate with the eggs.

4 Return the pan to medium-high heat and add the remaining 1 tablespoon grapeseed oil and then the green onions, pepper flakes, and the remaining 3 teaspoons ginger. Stir-fry until fragrant, about 30 seconds. Add the cabbage, and sprinkle with salt and black pepper. Stir to coat with the oil. Add the remaining 2 tablespoons water, cover the pan, and cook until the cabbage wilts, about 2 minutes. Add the egg and pork with any juices from the plate, the remaining 1 tablespoon soy sauce and 1 teaspoon sesame oil, and stir-fry until heated through. Transfer to a platter or shallow bowl.

5 To warm the tortillas, wrap them in barely damp paper towels, and then plastic wrap. Set on a plate and microwave on high for about 1 minute. Instruct diners to spread the hoisin mixture on each tortilla, fill with the pork mixture, roll up, and eat.

Pork loin cutlets or boneless chops, ½ lb (250 g), fat trimmed

Soy sauce, 3 tablespoons

Dry sherry, 1 tablespoon

Cornstarch, 1 teaspoon

Fresh ginger, 4 teaspoons minced

Hoisin sauce, 2 tablespoons

Asian sesame oil, 2 teaspoons

Water, 3 tablespoons

Grapeseed oil, 3 tablespoons

Large eggs, 2

Kosher salt and freshly ground black pepper

Green onions, 1 bunch, thinly sliced

Red pepper flakes, ¼ teaspoon

Shredded green cabbage, 1 package (1 lb/500 g)

Small soft corn tortillas, 8, or Mandarin pancakes

CLAMS
WITH BLACK BEAN SAUCE

MAKES 4-6 SERVINGS

Here, little clams are stir-fried with a bold Asian sauce that works doubletime as a seasoning, as well as an aid to steam the shells open. This dish comes together in minutes and looks and tastes like it came from an upscale Chinese restaurant. Serve with a side of hot cooked rice (see page 46).

1 In a bowl, stir together the broth, water, soy sauce, black beans, vinegar, sugar, pepper, and cornstarch. Set aside.

2 Warm a wok or large frying pan over medium-high heat, then swirl in the oil. Add 4 tablespoons (¾ oz/20 g) of the green onions, the ginger, garlic, and chile and stir-fry until fragrant, about 10 seconds. Add the sherry and stir-fry until most of the liquid has evaporated, about 30 seconds. Stir in the broth mixture, bring to a boil, and cook for about 30 seconds.

3 Add the clams to the pan, discarding any that do not close to the touch. Stir-fry until the clams are well coated with the sauce. Cover, reduce the heat to medium, and cook just until the shells open, 3–4 minutes.

4 Sprinkle the remaining 1 tablespoon green onions and the cilantro over the clams and stir-fry until heated through, about 1 minute longer. Discard any clams that failed to open. Transfer to a serving bowl and serve right away.

{ INGREDIENT DEMYSTIFIED: GREEN ONIONS
Green onions, aka scallions, have a narrow white base and long, flat green leaves. When called for in recipes, that usually means to use the white base along with the tender, light green parts of the leaves. The hairy tops and tough, dark green ends should be trimmed away and any slimy, browned layers pulled off before using.

Chicken broth, ⅓ cup (3 fl oz/80 ml)

Water, ⅓ cup (3 fl oz/80 ml)

Soy sauce, 2 tablespoons

Fermented black beans, 2 tablespoons, rinsed well and drained

Rice vinegar, ½ teaspoon

Sugar, 1 teaspoon

Freshly ground pepper, ⅛ teaspoon

Cornstarch, 1 teaspoon

Canola oil, 2 tablespoons

Green onions, 5 tablespoons (1 oz/30 g) minced

Fresh ginger, 2 tablespoons minced

Garlic, 3 cloves, minced

Red Fresno chile, 1, seeded and minced

Dry sherry, 2 tablespoons

Manila or littleneck clams, 2½ lb (1.25 kg), scrubbed

Fresh cilantro, 1 tablespoon chopped

GINGER SHRIMP *&* VEGETABLES

MAKES 4 SERVINGS

Stir-frying is perhaps one of the easiest techniques to use for making a quick one-pot meal. Start a pot of rice (see page 46) before you prep your ingredients, so the meal is all done at the same time. You can substitute small scallops for the shrimp, or leave them out entirely to make a vegetarian dish.

1 In a small bowl, whisk together the cornstarch, sherry, and water. Set aside.

2 Warm a wok or large frying pan over high heat, then swirl in 2 teaspoons of the grapeseed oil. Add the shrimp and stir-fry until bright pink but not yet cooked through, about 3 minutes. Do not overcook them. Transfer to a plate.

3 Return the pan to high heat. Drizzle in the remaining 2 teaspoons grapeseed oil. Add the ginger and garlic and stir-fry until fragrant, about 30 seconds. Add the snow peas and mushrooms, return the shrimp to the pan, and stir-fry until the snow peas are bright green, 30–60 seconds. Pour in the broth and cook until the shrimp are opaque throughout, 2–3 minutes longer.

4 Briefly stir the sherry mixture and then pour into the pan. Stir-fry until the sauce thickens and turns clear, about 2 minutes. Add the sesame oil and ¼ teaspoon salt, or more to taste, and season with pepper. Transfer to a serving dish and serve right away.

Cornstarch, 2 teaspoons

Dry sherry, 1 teaspoon

Water, 2 teaspoons

Grapeseed oil, 4 teaspoons

Large shrimp, 1 lb (500 g), peeled and deveined

Fresh ginger, 1 tablespoon minced

Garlic, 1 small clove, minced

Snow peas, 1 cup (3 oz/90 g), ends trimmed and strings removed

Cremini mushrooms, ½ lb (250 g), sliced

Chicken broth, ¼ cup (2 fl oz/60 ml)

Asian sesame oil, ¼ teaspoon

Kosher salt and freshly ground pepper

STIR-FRIED LEMONGRASS CHICKEN

Marinating the chicken for a few hours allows the fresh and spicy flavors to meld into the poultry. Be sure to get the wok and oil really hot, to help give the chicken a nice crisp crust. Serve this dish with steamed rice (see page 46) and garnish with basil for a fresh bite and colorful contrast.

1 In a mini food processor, combine the lemongrass, shallots, ginger, garlic, chile, 1 teaspoon salt, and 1 tablespoon of the oil and process until a smooth paste forms. Add 1–2 tablespoons water if needed to facilitate the grinding. Transfer the mixture to a large locking plastic bag, add the chicken cubes, and seal the bag. Turn the bag and gently massage the mixture into the chicken. Refrigerate for at least 4 hours or up to overnight.

2 In a small bowl, whisk together the soy sauce, fish sauce, vinegar, sugar, cornstarch, ⅛ teaspoon pepper, and 2 tablespoons water. Set aside.

3 Warm a wok or large frying pan over medium-high heat, then swirl in 2 tablespoons of the oil. Add the onion and stir-fry until tender and lightly browned, 7–8 minutes. Transfer the onion to a bowl. Set the pan aside.

4 Remove the chicken from the marinade in the bag and pat dry with paper towels. Discard the marinade. Return the pan to high heat and add the remaining 2 tablespoons oil. When the oil is hot and shimmering, working in batches if necessary, add the chicken cubes and stir-fry until golden brown, 4–5 minutes.

5 Return the onions to the pan. Pour in the soy–fish sauce mixture and stir-fry until the sauce thickens and the chicken is opaque throughout, 1–2 minutes. Divide the chicken among individual bowls, sprinkle with the basil, and serve right away.

Lemongrass, 2 stalks, white part only, chopped

Shallots, 2, roughly chopped

Fresh ginger, 2 tablespoons roughly chopped

Garlic, 3 cloves, roughly chopped

Jalapeño chile, 1, seeded and roughly chopped

Kosher salt and freshly ground pepper

Canola oil, 5 tablespoons (3 fl oz/80 ml)

Water, as needed

Skinless, boneless chicken thighs, 1½ lb (750 g), cut into 1-inch (2.5-cm) cubes

Soy sauce, 4 teaspoons

Asian fish sauce, 1 tablespoon

Rice vinegar, 1 teaspoon

Sugar, ½ teaspoon

Cornstarch, ½ teaspoon

Small yellow onion, 1, halved and thinly sliced

Fresh basil, 2 tablespoons torn leaves

TANGERINE BEEF

MAKES 4-6 SERVINGS

This dish tastes even better at home than in a restaurant and it cooks up in minutes. Stir-frying with citrus juice adds a nice, tangy glaze to the ingredients in the wok. The steak can be substituted by 1-inch (2.5-cm) chunks of skinless chicken breast, if desired. Serve with hot cooked rice (see page 46).

1 Cut the flank steak across the grain into slices ⅛ inch (3 mm) thick. In a large bowl, combine ½ teaspoon of the sugar, the baking soda, and 1 teaspoon salt and stir to mix well. Add the beef slices and stir to coat thoroughly. Let stand at room temperature for 30 minutes.

2 In a small bowl, stir together the tangerine zest and juice, sherry, hoisin sauce, soy sauce, chile bean paste, ginger, sesame oil, cornstarch, and the remaining ¼ teaspoon sugar until the sugar and cornstarch dissolve. Set aside.

3 Pat the beef slices dry with paper towels. Warm a wok or large frying pan over high heat, then swirl in 2 tablespoons of the canola oil. Add half of the beef in a single layer and sear until brown on the first side, about 1 minute. Using tongs, turn and sear until brown on the second side, about 30 seconds. Transfer the meat to a colander to drain. Return the pan to high heat, warm 1 tablespoon of the oil, and repeat to sear the remaining beef. Transfer the second batch to the colander to drain.

4 Wipe the pan clean. Reheat over high heat and add the remaining 1 tablespoon oil. When the oil is hot, add the onion and bell pepper and stir-fry until the edges begin to brown, 3–4 minutes. Add the chile and garlic and stir-fry for 1 minute. Pour in the tangerine juice mixture and return the beef to the pan. Stir-fry until the sauce thickens and the beef is heated through, about 1 minute. Transfer to a bowl or platter and serve right away.

Flank steak, 1½ lb (750 g)

Sugar, ¾ teaspoon

Baking soda, ¼ teaspoon

Kosher salt

Tangerine or orange zest, 1 teaspoon finely grated

Fresh tangerine or orange juice, ¼ cup (2 fl oz/60 ml)

Dry sherry, 1 tablespoon

Hoisin sauce, 1 tablespoon

Soy sauce, ¼ cup (2 fl oz/60 ml)

Chile bean paste, 1 teaspoon

Fresh ginger, 1 teaspoon minced

Asian sesame oil, ½ teaspoon

Cornstarch, ¼ teaspoon

Canola oil, 4 tablespoons (2 fl oz/60 ml)

Small yellow onion, 1, halved and thinly sliced

Small green bell pepper, 1, seeded and thinly sliced lengthwise

Red Fresno chile, 1, seeded and thinly sliced lengthwise

Garlic, 2 cloves, minced

CASHEW BROCCOLI

MAKES 4 SERVINGS

To make this dish fully vegetarian, simply omit the oyster sauce. Or, for meat lovers, add some leftover chicken or beef with the soy sauce in step 3. To customize the dish even more, switch up the nuts, using walnuts or almonds if you prefer. If serving this as a main dish for two, serve over hot cooked rice (below).

1 Preheat the oven to 375°F (190°C). Pour the cashews onto a rimmed baking sheet. Toast the cashews in the oven until they turn a shade or two darker and are fragrant, 6–8 minutes. Pour onto a plate to cool.

2 In a small bowl, stir together the broth, oyster sauce, soy sauce, sherry, and cornstarch.

3 Warm a wok or a large frying pan over medium-high heat, then swirl in the oil. Add the broccoli and stir-fry until the broccoli is well coated with oil and is vibrant green, about 3 minutes. Add the garlic and stir-fry for 1 minute. Add the soy sauce mixture, bring to a boil, and stir-fry until the sauce thickens and the broccoli is tender-crisp, about 4 minutes.

4 Add the cashews to the pan and stir well. Transfer to a serving dish and serve right away.

Cashews, ½ cup (3 oz/90 g)

Chicken broth, ½ cup (4 fl oz/125 ml)

Oyster sauce, 2 tablespoons

Soy sauce, 2 tablespoons

Dry sherry, 2 tablespoons

Cornstarch, 1 teaspoon

Canola oil, 2 tablespoons

Broccoli, 1 head (about 1 lb/500 g), cut into 1-inch (2.5-cm) florets

Garlic, 1 clove, minced

{ **HOW TO COOK RICE** In a small saucepan with a tight-fitting lid, combine 2 parts water to 1 part rice. Bring the water to a boil over high heat, then reduce the heat to low, cover, and cook until the rice is tender and the liquid is absorbed, about 20 minutes for white rice and about 50 minutes for brown rice. Let the rice stand with the lid on for 10 minutes. Before serving, fluff the grains with a fork. Start with 1 cup rice and you end up with 3 cups cooked rice, enough for 4–6 servings.

CHICKEN & VEGETABLE FRIED RICE

MAKES 4-6 SERVINGS

Stir-frying cooked rice over high heat gives it a crisp texture and golden hue. You can vary the other ingredients to suit your taste. To prevent the rice from sticking when stir-fried, cook it ahead of time, spread it out on a baking sheet, and let it cool completely.

1   Bring a saucepan of water to a boil. Add 1 teaspoon salt and the chicken and return just to a boil, then quickly reduce the heat to medium and simmer, uncovered, until the chicken is opaque throughout, 10–15 minutes. Using tongs, transfer the chicken to a plate until cool enough to handle. Shred the chicken.

2   In a small bowl, stir together the soy sauce, fish sauce, and lime juice. Set aside.

3   Warm a large wok or frying pan over medium-high heat, then swirl in 2 tablespoons of the oil. Add the shallots, ginger, and garlic and stir-fry until fragrant, about 10 seconds. Add the cabbage and carrots and stir-fry until the cabbage begins to wilt, about 3 minutes. Add the chicken and stir-fry until heated through, about 1 minute. Transfer to a bowl.

4   Wipe the pan clean. Place the pan over high heat, and swirl in the remaining 1 tablespoon oil. Add the eggs and scramble until just set. Add the rice and stir-fry for 1 minute, using a spatula to break up any large chunks. Stir in the peas, return the chicken mixture to the pan, and stir-fry until the rice is heated through, about 5 minutes. Pour in the soy-lime mixture and toss and stir until the rice absorbs the sauce, about 3 minutes longer. Transfer to individual bowls and serve right away.

Ingredients

Kosher salt

Skinless, boneless chicken breasts, ¼ lb (125 g)

Soy sauce, 2 tablespoons

Asian fish sauce, 1½ tablespoons

Fresh lime juice, 1 tablespoon

Canola oil, 3 tablespoons

Shallots, 3, minced

Fresh ginger, 1 tablespoon minced

Garlic, 2 cloves, minced

Napa cabbage, ½ small head, trimmed, cored, and cut into ½-inch (12-mm) pieces

Carrots, 2, chopped

Large eggs, 3, lightly beaten

Cooked white rice, 3 cups (15 oz/470 g), cooled completely (page 46)

Frozen peas, ⅓ cup (1½ oz/45 g), thawed

PAD THAI

It's safe to say that making homemade pad thai could be life changing.
Planned correctly, the whole dish comes together in about 30 minutes,
and tastes infinitely better than takeout. The noodles and fish sauce can
be found in the international foods aisle of grocery stores or at Asian markets.

1 Bring a saucepan three-fourths full of water to a rolling boil, then remove from the heat. Drop the noodles into the water and stir well. Let the noodles stand until tender, about 30 minutes. Drain well.

2 In a small bowl, combine the fish sauce, lime juice, and sugar and stir with a fork to dissolve the sugar. Set aside.

3 Warm a wok or large frying pan over high heat, then swirl in the canola oil. Add the shrimp, garlic, and pepper flakes and stir-fry until fragrant, about 1 minute. Pour in the eggs and let them cook, without stirring, until lightly set, about 30 seconds. Then, stir well to scramble the eggs with the shrimp. Add the fish sauce mixture and drained noodles and cook, lifting and stirring the noodles constantly, until the ingredients are well blended, about 2 minutes. Stir in 1 cup (2 oz/60 g) of the bean sprouts, 2 tablespoons of the nuts, and 2 tablespoons of the green onions, and cook, stirring, until heated through and evenly distributed, about 1 minute longer.

4 Transfer the noodles to a platter. Garnish with the cilantro, mint, remaining bean sprouts, peanuts, and green onions. Serve right away.

Dry flat rice noodles,
¼ inch (6 mm) wide,
1 package (7 oz/220 g)

Asian fish sauce, ¼ cup
(2 fl oz/60 ml)

Fresh lime juice,
2 tablespoons

Sugar, 2 tablespoons

Canola oil, 2 tablespoons

Medium shrimp, ½ lb
(250 g), peeled and deveined

Garlic, 3 cloves, minced

Red pepper flakes,
¼ teaspoon

Large eggs, 3, lightly beaten

Bean sprouts, 2 cups
(4 oz/120 g)

Unsalted roasted peanuts,
4 tablespoons (1 oz/30 g),
chopped

Green onions, 4 tablespoons
(¾ oz/20 g) thinly sliced

Fresh cilantro, ½ cup
(¾ oz/20 g) chopped

Fresh mint, ¼ cup
(⅓ oz/10 g) chopped

{ INGREDIENT DEMYSTIFIED:
FISH SAUCE If you've never used fish sauce before, don't be alarmed by the smell. Right out of the bottle, it's stinky stuff, but it adds surprising depth of flavor to dishes. In Southeast Asia, they use fish sauce in the same way Westerners use salt, both as a cooking seasoning and at the table. The clear liquid ranges from amber to dark brown.

STIR-FRIED ZUCCHINI & SHIITAKES

Tender zucchini and meaty shiitake mushrooms are amped up with bold
Asian condiments and crunchy sesame seeds. Purple cabbage and red bell
pepper, cut into uniform slices, can substitute for the vegetables in this recipe.
Add diced tofu for added protein and serve over rice (see page 46).

1 Remove and discard the stems from the shiitake mushrooms. Cut the
caps into slices ¼ inch (6 mm) thick. Trim the ends of the zucchini
and cut each in half lengthwise. Cut each zucchini half crosswise
into slices ¼ inch (6 mm) thick. Set the vegetables aside.

2 Heat a small dry frying pan over medium heat. Add the sesame seeds
and toast, stirring occasionally, until golden brown, 4–5 minutes.
Immediately transfer to a small plate and set aside.

3 In a small bowl, stir together the soy sauce, vinegar, sesame oil,
and sugar and set aside.

4 Warm a wok or large frying pan over high heat, then swirl in
2 tablespoons of the canola oil. When the oil is hot, add the
mushrooms and stir-fry until they release their juices, 4–5 minutes.
Transfer to a large bowl. Return the pan to high heat and warm
the remaining 1 tablespoon canola oil. Add the zucchini and stir-fry
until golden brown and just tender, 7–8 minutes. Add the green
onions and garlic and stir-fry until fragrant, about 1 minute.

5 Return the mushrooms to the pan and pour in the soy-vinegar mixture.
Stir-fry until the vegetables are heated through and most of the sauce
has evaporated, about 2 minutes. Transfer the vegetables to a bowl,
garnish with the toasted sesame seeds, and serve right away.

Shiitake mushrooms,
½ lb (250 g)

Zucchini, 1½ lb (750 g)

Sesame seeds, 1 teaspoon

Soy sauce, 2 tablespoons

Rice vinegar, 1 tablespoon

Asian sesame oil,
2 teaspoons

Sugar, ½ teaspoon

Canola oil, 3 tablespoons

Green onions, 2, minced

Garlic, 2 cloves, minced

FRY

ALL ABOUT
FRYING

Frying, or more specifically deep-frying, means to cook foods either fully or partially submerged in hot oil. The oil is heated to a specific temperature that is best suited to the specific type of food. Some foods, such as potatoes, can be added directly to the hot oil to gain a crisp finish. Others, such as vegetables or fish, are first either coated with flour or a batter to help protect the delicate ingredients from the hot oil and ensure a crunchy texture.

Deep-frying refers to cooking food in a large amount of very hot oil. The oil creates a crisp, golden crust that seals in natural juices, keeping food moist and tender.

With oil temperatures just shy of 400°F (200°C), frying can be dangerous work, but if you choose the right equipment and take care with what you're doing, it isn't difficult. On the contrary, frying is easy to master. Choose a sturdy, heavy-bottomed saucepan or stockpot with high sides to help control spattering. Experienced fryers can also use a well-made sauté pan. Choose a neutral-flavored cooking oil that can withstand high cooking temperatures, such as peanut or canola oil.

Frying goes quickly and requires consistent attention throughout the cooking process. Be sure that your ingredients are prepped and assembled near the stove and your kitchen ventilation is turned on before starting.

FRY TERM CONFUSION

Frying, deep-frying, shallow-frying, and pan-frying are all terms you see in cookbooks and magazines and they can be confusing. Technically, they are all slightly different. Deep-frying means to submerge foods completely in hot oil, while shallow-frying uses much less oil. Pan-frying is similar to sautéing.

LARGE, DEEP SAUCEPAN

SET OF RESTAURANT-STYLE TONGS

WIRE SKIMMER

DEEP-FRYING THERMOMETER

OIL WITH A HIGH SMOKE POINT

MEDIUM-HIGH TO HIGH HEAT

SECRETS TO SUCCESS

HEAT SMARTLY
Always heat oil to the temperature listed in the recipe (overheated oil can combust) and regulate the heat throughout the frying process to be sure it stays relatively consistent.

DON'T OVERHEAT
Take care not to let the oil heat past about 400°F (200°C), as it is can be dangerous. If the temp starts to creep up too high, remove the oil from the heat and let it stand undisturbed to cool down to a safe cooking temperature.

COOK ASAP Try not to let breaded or battered foods sit for too long before frying or they will become soggy.

SEASON WELL
Season fried foods while they're still hot, ideally while they are draining, for the best flavor.

FRY IN SMALL BATCHES This helps foods cook evenly and develop the desired crisp crust. Keep batches warm in a 200°F (95°C) oven as you work. Be sure to return the oil to the proper temperature before adding the next batch.

BE SAFE & SENSIBLE Let the oil cool completely before discarding it. Consult your local community regulations for the best way to discard used oil.

KEEPING FRIED FOODS CRISP

Set up a draining station before you begin to fry: Line a rimmed baking sheet with a few layers of paper towels, then place a wire cooling rack on top of the paper towel–lined baking sheet. Using tongs or a wire skimmer, transfer the food from the hot oil to the cooling station. Any leftover oil will fall through the rack onto the paper towels below, helping the fried food stay crisp.

HOW TO
FRY

1
POUR IN THE OIL
Pour oil with a high smoke
point into a wide, heavy,
deep-sided saucepan to
the depth indicated in the recipe

2
TAKE THE TEMPERATURE
Clip a deep-frying thermometer
onto the edge of the pan and warm
over medium-high or high heat.
Watch closely until it reaches
the desired temperature.

3
BATTER THE FOOD
If called for in the recipe,
plunge the food into a batter
or breading. Coat only enough
food for 1 batch of frying.

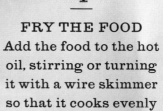

4

FRY THE FOOD
Add the food to the hot
oil, stirring or turning
it with a wire skimmer
so that it cooks evenly

5

DRAIN THE FAT
Using a wire skimmer or tongs,
transfer the food to the draining
station to dry. Re-warm the
oil to the desired temperature
between batches, if necessary.

CINNAMON-SUGAR DOUGHNUTS

MAKES ABOUT 1 DOZEN DOUGHNUTS AND HOLES

Doughnuts are the perfect group cooking project. Have your friends set up an assembly line: there should be a dough making and cutting station, a safe, well-protected area for frying, a draining station, and a toppings station. Once the doughnuts have been cooled and coated in cinnamon-sugar, enjoy them right away.

1 Pour the oil to a depth of at least 1 inch (2.5 cm) into a deep, heavy pot and warm over medium-high heat to 375°F (190°C) on a deep-frying thermometer. Make sure the pot is no more than half full. Put a large rack on a large rimmed baking sheet and place near the stove.

2 Meanwhile, in a bowl, stir together the flour, sugar, baking powder, salt, baking soda, and nutmeg. In another bowl, whisk together the egg, buttermilk, cider, melted butter, and vanilla until smooth. Add the egg mixture to the flour mixture and stir until the dough is thick.

3 With floured hands, transfer the dough to a floured work surface, and knead lightly until the ingredients are evenly mixed. The dough will be loose and sticky. Pat the dough into a disk 1 inch (2.5 cm) thick. Flour a doughnut cutter 2¼ inches (5.5 cm) in diameter and cut out the doughnuts, flouring the cutter as needed to prevent sticking. Or, use 2 round biscuit cutters, 2¼ inches (5.5 cm) and 1¼ inches (3 cm) in diameter. Scraps can be patted into a disk and cut again.

4 Using a flat spatula, carefully slide the doughnuts and holes, 2 or 3 at a time, into the hot oil. Fry until golden on the undersides, about 1 minute. Using a wire skimmer, flip them over and fry on the other side until golden, 1–2 minutes. If darkening too quickly, reduce the heat slightly. With the skimmer, transfer the doughnuts to the rack to drain.

5 While the doughnuts are still warm, mix the ½ cup (4 oz/125 g) sugar with the cinnamon in a paper bag. Add the doughnuts, and shake gently to coat. Serve warm or at room temperature.

Canola oil, for frying

All-purpose flour, 2¾ cups (14 oz/440 g), plus more for dusting

Sugar, ¼ cup (2 oz/60 g), plus ½ cup (4 oz/125 g), for topping

Baking powder, 1 tablespoon

Kosher salt, 1 teaspoon

Baking soda, ½ teaspoon

Nutmeg, ⅛ teaspoon, freshly grated

Large egg, 1

Buttermilk, ½ cup (4 fl oz/125 ml)

Apple cider, ¼ cup (2 fl oz/60 ml)

Unsalted butter, 2 tablespoons, melted

Pure vanilla extract, ½ teaspoon

Ground cinnamon, 2 teaspoons

ULTIMATE FRENCH FRIES WITH SPICY KETCHUP

MAKES 6 SERVINGS

You can make restaurant-quality french fries at home with just 3 ingredients: potatoes, salt, and oil. The secret to crisp, perfectly cooked fries is to soak the raw potatoes in water to remove excess starch, and then fry them twice. Smoky chipotles and spicy jalapeños add a whole new flavor dimension to plain old ketchup.

1 To make the ketchup, in a small saucepan over medium heat, warm the oil. Add the chipotle and jalapeño chiles, onion, and garlic and sauté until softened, 4–5 minutes. Reduce the heat to low and stir in the ketchup, sugar, cumin, and chili powder. Simmer until the mixture is deep red in color and the flavors are blended, about 15 minutes. Let cool, then refrigerate until ready to use.

2 Peel the potatoes, or leave the peels on. Using a sharp knife, cut a thin slice from the potatoes so that they lay flat on the board. Cut the potatoes lengthwise into slices ¼–½ inch (6–12 mm) thick. Arrange the slices flat on the cutting board and cut them into ¼- to ½-inch (6- to 12-mm) strips. Place the potato strips in a large bowl of salted water and let stand for at least 1 hour or for up to 3 hours. Drain the potatoes well and pat completely dry with paper towels.

3 Pour the oil to a depth of 4–5 inches (10–13 cm) into a deep, heavy saucepan and heat over medium heat to 325°F (165°C) on a deep-frying thermometer. Line a baking sheet with paper towels.

4 Working in batches, add the potatoes to the hot oil, being careful not to crowd the pan. Fry the potatoes, stirring once or twice with a wire skimmer, until they are almost tender but still pale and waxy, 6–8 minutes. Using the skimmer, transfer the potatoes to the baking sheet. Let stand for at least 5 minutes or for up to 3 hours.

5 Just before serving, reheat the oil to 375°F (190°C). Line another baking sheet with paper towels. Working in batches, deep-fry the potatoes until golden brown, 1–2 minutes. Using a slotted spoon, transfer the potatoes to the baking sheet to drain briefly. Season with salt and serve right away with the ketchup.

FOR THE SPICY KETCHUP

Olive oil, 1 tablespoon

Canned chipotle chiles in adobo sauce, 4, chopped

Jalapeño chile, 1, seeded and chopped

Small yellow onion, 1, diced

Garlic, 2 cloves, minced

Ketchup, 1 cup (8 oz/250 g)

Sugar, 1 tablespoon

Ground cumin, 1 teaspoon

Chili powder, 1 teaspoon

Russet potatoes, 4–6, about 2 lb (1 kg) total weight

Peanut or canola oil, for frying

Flaky sea salt or kosher salt, for sprinkling

JALAPEÑO POPPERS

MAKES 12 SMALL POPPERS

What's a better use for a chile then to stuff it with a creamy bacon and cheese mixture, dip it in batter, and deep-fry it? These poppers are the real deal: perfect for game day, parties, or just as a snack to be enjoyed with an ice-cold beer.

1 Using the tip of a paring knife, slit each jalapeño on one side from the stem to the tip, then make a partial cut at the base of the stem, leaving the stem end intact. Gently open up the chile and remove the seeds with the knife or a small spoon.

2 In a small bowl, mix together the bacon, cream cheese, Cheddar, Monterey jack, and hot-pepper sauce until well blended. Season with salt and pepper. Using a small spoon, fill the chiles with the cheese mixture, dividing it evenly. Close the filled chiles, pressing firmly on the seams so they retain their shape.

3 In a shallow bowl, whisk together the eggs and milk. In a second shallow bowl, stir together the panko and a pinch each of salt and pepper. One at a time, dip the filled chiles into the egg mixture, allow the excess to drip off, then dip into the bread crumbs, patting gently to help them adhere. Transfer to a baking sheet. Let dry for about 10 minutes, then repeat, dipping the chiles first in the egg mixture and then in the crumbs to form a second coating.

4 Pour the oil to a depth of at least 3 inches (7.5 cm) into a deep, heavy saucepan and heat over medium-high heat to 325°F (165°C) on a deep-frying thermometer. Preheat the oven to 200°F (95°C). Line a rimmed baking sheet with paper towels.

5 Working in batches, add the stuffed, breaded jalapeños to the hot oil, being careful not to crowd the pan. Fry, stirring occasionally with a wire skimmer, until the jalapeños are golden brown, about 6 minutes. Using the skimmer, transfer the jalapeños to paper towels to drain and keep warm in the oven while you fry the remaining ones. Serve warm.

Small jalapeño chiles, 12

Applewood-smoked bacon, 2 thick slices, finely chopped and fried until crisp

Cream cheese, 4 oz (125 g), at room temperature

Sharp Cheddar cheese, ½ cup (2 oz/60 g) finely shredded

Monterey jack cheese, ½ cup (2 oz/60 g) finely shredded

Hot pepper sauce, 1 teaspoon

Kosher salt and freshly ground pepper

Large eggs, 2

Whole milk, 1 tablespoon

Panko bread crumbs, 1 cup (1½ oz/45 g)

Canola oil, for frying

CORN FRITTERS WITH LIME

These delish little patties come together in minutes with just a little preparation. You really want to use fresh corn here, as frozen corn won't produce the same crunch. Remember this recipe in the late summer and fall when corn season is in full swing.

1 In a small bowl, stir together the corn kernels and lime juice. In a medium bowl, whisk together the milk, egg, and butter. In a large bowl, stir together the flour, cornmeal, baking powder, salt, and cayenne. Quickly mix the egg mixture into the flour mixture until smooth. Fold in the corn mixture, green onion, cilantro (if using), and cheddar cheese.

2 Pour the oil to a depth of 1 inch (2.5 cm) into a deep saucepan and warm over medium-high heat to 375°F (190°C) on a deep-frying thermometer. Put a large wire rack on a large rimmed baking sheet and place near the stove.

3 Working in batches, drop the batter by heaping tablespoons into the hot oil, being careful not to crowd the pan. Fry until browned on one side, about 2 minutes. Using a wire skimmer, flip the fritters over and fry until golden, puffed, and cooked through, 2–3 minutes longer. Using the skimmer, transfer to the rack to drain.

4 Transfer the hot fritters to a paper towel–lined platter and serve right away with the lime wedges for squeezing.

{ **PREP WORK: REMOVING CORN KERNELS FROM THE COB**
Hold a shucked corn ear in both hands and quickly but firmly break the cob in half crosswise. Hold each cob half upright, flat end down, on a cutting board with your nondominant hand. Using a sharp knife, cut straight down between the kernels and the cob, but not too deeply, to avoid the kernels' fibrous bases. Let the corn kernels fall on the cutting board.

Fresh corn kernels, 1½ cups (9 oz/280 g) (from about 3 ears), chopped

Fresh lime juice, 2 teaspoons

Whole milk, ½ cup (4 fl oz/125 ml)

Large egg, 1

Unsalted butter, 2 tablespoons, melted and cooled

All-purpose flour, ¾ cup (4 oz/125 g)

Fine-grind cornmeal, ¼ cup (1½ oz/45 g)

Baking powder, 1 teaspoon

Kosher salt, ¾ teaspoon

Cayenne pepper, ⅛ teaspoon

Green onion, 1 tablespoon chopped

Fresh cilantro, 1 tablespoon chopped (optional)

Cheddar cheese, ¼ cup (1 oz/30 g) shredded

Canola oil, for frying

Lime wedges, for serving

BEER-BATTERED ONION RINGS

MAKES 4–6 SERVINGS

You don't need fancy equipment to make awesome onion rings—just a knife, a heavy saucepan, a thermometer, and a metal skimmer. If you don't have a metal rack for cooling, drain them on cut-up paper grocery bags; just be sure they don't sit for too long. A little flaky salt lends a nice crunch and makes the onion rings look beautiful.

1 In a bowl, whisk together the flour, egg, ½ teaspoon salt, and the cayenne pepper. Add the beer and whisk just until combined. Do not worry if the batter has a few lumps. Let stand for 30 minutes.

2 Meanwhile, cut the onions into thick rounds, and separate the rounds into rings.

3 Pour the oil to a depth of at least 3 inches (7.5 cm) into a large, heavy saucepan and heat over high heat to 350°F (180°C) on a deep-frying thermometer. Preheat the oven to 200°F (95°C). Set a large wire rack on a large rimmed baking sheet and place near the stove.

4 Working in batches, dip the onion rings into the batter to coat, letting the excess batter drip back into the bowl, and carefully add to the hot oil, being careful not to crowd the pan. Fry until golden brown, about 3 minutes. Using a wire skimmer, transfer to the rack and keep warm in the oven while you fry the remaining onion rings.

5 Sprinkle the onion rings with flaky salt, then transfer them to a platter. Serve right away with ketchup, if desired.

Cake flour, 1 cup (4 oz/125 g)

Large egg, 1

Kosher salt

Cayenne pepper, ¼ teaspoon

Lager beer, ¾ cup (6 fl oz/180 ml)

Yellow onions, 2 large (about 1 lb/500 g total weight)

Canola oil, for frying

Flaky sea salt or kosher salt, for sprinkling

Ketchup, for serving (optional)

{ **MORE FRIED VEGETABLES, PLEASE!** This batter also works well with other vegetables. Try broccoli or cauliflower florets, whole mushrooms, or thawed frozen artichoke hearts. Serve with salt and lemon wedges for squeezing.

FRITTO MISTO

This popular Italian dish translates to "mixed fry" in Italian. Instead of
a batter, the ingredients are coated with a dusting of flour, producing a
featherlight crust. Serve with a side of garlic mayo (page 124), if desired.
Ask for cleaned squid at the fishmonger so you don't have to deal with the mess.

1 Rinse the squid and shrimp, drain well, and pat dry with paper towels.
Cut the squid bodies into rings ½ inch (12 mm) wide and the tentacles
into bite-sized pieces. Cut 1 lemon crosswise into very thin slices and
remove the seeds. Cut the second lemon into wedges and set aside.
In a bowl, toss together the flour and a pinch of salt.

2 Pour the oil to a depth of 3 inches (7.5 cm) into a deep, heavy frying
pan and heat over high heat to 375°F (190°C) on a deep-frying
thermometer. Preheat the oven to 200°F (95°C). Line a large
ovenproof platter with paper towels and place near the stove.

3 Add about one-fourth each of the seafood, lemon slices, and zucchini
to the flour and toss until lightly coated. Lift from the flour, shaking
off the excess, and carefully ease the pieces, a few at a time, into
the hot oil. Fry until the shrimp turn pink and the other ingredients
are pale gold, about 3 minutes. Using a wire skimmer, transfer the
seafood, lemon slices, and zucchini to the towel-lined platter to drain,
and place in the oven to keep warm. Repeat to fry the remaining
ingredients in 3 batches, allowing the oil to return to 375°F (190°C)
between batches.

4 Transfer the fried seafood, zucchini, and lemon slices to a clean
platter, if desired. Sprinkle with flaky salt and serve right away
with the lemon wedges for squeezing.

Cleaned squid (tentacles and bodies), ½ lb (250 g)

Medium shrimp, ½ lb (250 g), peeled and deveined with tail segments intact

Lemons, 2

All-purpose flour, 1 cup (5 oz/155 g)

Kosher salt

Canola or peanut oil, for frying

Small zucchini, 2, ends trimmed, cut into sticks about 2 inches (5 cm) long by ¼ inch (6 mm) wide and thick

Flaky sea salt or kosher salt, for sprinkling

CHICKEN TAQUITOS

MAKES 4–6 SERVINGS

Crisp tortilla tubes filled with seasoned chicken and dipped in creamy guacamole—what more could you want? The taquitos can be filled up to 45 minutes before frying, if covered in plastic wrap and kept at room temperature. If you like, serve them on a bed of shredded cabbage tossed with fresh lime juice.

1 In a frying pan over medium heat, warm the 1 tablespoon oil. Add the onion, chile, and garlic and sauté just until softened, about 3 minutes. Raise the heat to medium-high, add the tomato, and cook, stirring occasionally, until most of the excess moisture is absorbed, 10–15 minutes. Remove from the heat and stir in the chicken. Season to taste with salt. Set aside.

2 Pour about 3 tablespoons oil into a deep, heavy frying pan over medium-high heat. When the oil is hot but not smoking, pass each tortilla briefly through it, turning once. Transfer to paper towels to drain.

3 To form each taquito, put a large spoonful of the filling along the center of a tortilla, roll it up tightly, and secure with a wooden toothpick.

4 Pour the oil to a depth of 1 inch (2.5 cm) into the frying pan and warm over medium-high heat to 350°F (180°C) on a deep-frying thermometer. Preheat the oven to 200°F (95°C). Line a large ovenproof platter with paper towels.

5 Working in batches, add the taquitos to the oil and fry, turning several times, until lightly browned and crisp, about 2 minutes. Using tongs, lift the taquitos out of the oil, allowing any excess oil to run off, and transfer to the towel-lined platter to drain. Place them in the oven to keep warm while you fry the rest of the taquitos.

6 Arrange the taquitos on a platter, sprinkle with salt, and serve right away with the guacamole and sour cream.

Canola oil, 1 tablespoon, plus more for frying

White onion, ½ cup (2 oz/60 g) chopped

Jalapeño chile, 1, seeded and minced

Garlic, 1 clove, minced

Large, ripe tomato, 1, finely chopped

Cooked, shredded chicken, 2½ cups (15 oz/470 g)

Kosher salt

Corn tortillas, 12, about 6 inches (15 cm) in diameter

Guacamole and sour cream, for serving

VEGETABLE TEMPURA

MAKES 4 SERVINGS

Tempura is a classic Japanese dish of fried, batter-coated vegetables
or seafood. The key to achieving the unique fluffy-yet-crisp coating is using
a chilled batter made with ice water. The 3-ingredient dipping sauce
is addictive, so you might want to make a double batch.

FOR THE DIPPING SAUCE
Soy sauce, 3 tablespoons
Mirin, 3 tablespoons
Sugar, 1 teaspoon

Cake flour, 1 cup (4 oz/125 g)
Rice flour, 1 cup (5 oz/155 g)
Kosher salt, 1 teaspoon
Baking soda, ¼ teaspoon
Large egg yolks, 2
Ice water, 1½ cups
(12 fl oz/375 ml)
Canola oil, for frying
Carrot, 1, cut into pieces
4 inches (10 cm) long by
¼ inch (6 mm) thick
Zucchini, 1, cut into pieces
4 inches (10 cm) long by
¼ inch (6 mm) thick
Small sweet potato, 1,
peeled, halved, and cut into
pieces 4 inches (10 cm) long
by ⅛ inch (3 mm) thick
Green beans, 3 oz (90 g),
trimmed
Shiitake mushrooms,
5, stems removed and caps
cut in half

1 To make the dipping sauce, stir together the soy sauce, mirin, and sugar until the sugar dissolves. Set aside.

2 Set a fine-mesh sieve over a bowl. Pour the cake and rice flours, salt, and baking soda into the sieve to sift them into the bowl. In another bowl, using a fork, beat together the egg yolks and ice water until blended. Stir the egg yolk mixture into the dry ingredients just until the batter comes together.

3 Pour the oil to a depth of 3 inches (7.5 cm) into a deep, heavy saucepan, and warm over high heat to 375°F (190°C) on a deep-frying thermometer. Preheat the oven to 200°F (95°C).

4 Using tongs, dip a carrot piece into the batter, letting the excess drip back into the bowl. Slide the carrot into the hot oil. Repeat to add 4 or 5 more assorted vegetable pieces to the oil; do not crowd the pan. Fry, gently and carefully moving the pieces back and forth with a wire skimmer, until light golden brown, 1–2 minutes. Using the skimmer, transfer the vegetables to paper towels to drain. Arrange the fried tempura on an ovenproof platter and keep warm in the oven while you fry the remaining vegetables. Allow the oil to return to 375°F (190°C) and skim off any browned bits of batter from the oil between batches.

5 Serve the tempura right away with the dipping sauce.

FRIED FISH TACOS

MAKES 4 SERVINGS

We like our fish tacos Baja-style: coated with a beer batter and deep-fried, then popped into warm corn tortillas along with crunchy shredded cabbage and homemade taco sauce. Top them off with a squeeze of fresh lime juice. The fish should be served as soon as possible after frying; if it sits for too long the crust gets soggy.

1 In a bowl, stir together the flour, 1 teaspoon of the garlic salt, and ½ teaspoon of the cayenne pepper. Pour in the beer and whisk until smooth. Cover and let stand for at least 10 minutes or for up to 1 hour.

2 In a small bowl, stir together the ketchup, mayonnaise, and yogurt until blended. Set aside.

3 Cut the fish into 8 strips, each about 4 inches (10 cm) long and ¾ inch (2 cm) wide, and place in a nonreactive bowl. Sprinkle with the lime juice, the remaining ½ teaspoon garlic salt, and the remaining ¼ teaspoon cayenne and toss to mix. Let marinate at room temperature for 10 minutes.

4 Pour the oil to a depth of 1 inch (2.5 cm) into a deep, heavy frying pan and warm over medium-high heat to 375°F (190°C) on a deep-frying thermometer. Pat the fish dry with paper towels. One at a time, dip a strip into the batter to coat, allowing the excess to drip off, and carefully add the battered fish to the hot oil. Do not allow the pieces to touch. Deep-fry, turning once with a wire skimmer, until the strips are crisp and golden, about 7 minutes. Using the skimmer, transfer to paper towels to drain.

5 Transfer the fried fish to a warmed serving plate. Serve the warmed tortillas, ketchup-mayo sauce, cilantro, cabbage, and lime wedges in separate dishes and have diners assemble their own tacos.

All-purpose flour, 1 cup
(5 oz/155 g)

Garlic salt, 1½ teaspoon

Cayenne pepper, ¾ teaspoon

Dark beer, 1 cup
(8 fl oz/250 ml)

Ketchup, ⅓ cup (3 oz/90 g)

Mayonnaise, ⅓ cup
(3 fl oz/80 ml)

Plain yogurt, ⅓ cup
(3 oz/90 g)

Skinless red snapper or
sea bass fillets, ¾ lb (375 g)

Fresh lime juice, 1 teaspoon

Canola oil, for frying

Small corn tortillas, 8,
warmed

Chopped fresh cilantro,
shredded red cabbage, and
lime wedges, for serving

SPICY BUTTERMILK FRIED CHICKEN

MAKES 4 SERVINGS

The key to moist and flavorful fried chicken is to soak the chicken in a salt solution, or brine, for a few hours before frying. Here, the brine also includes tangy buttermilk, herbs, garlic, and cayenne pepper for extra flavor and juiciness. Serve with hot-pepper sauce on the side, if desired.

1 In a large bowl, whisk together the buttermilk and ⅓ cup (2 oz/60 g) salt. Crush the herbs well with your fingers. Whisk the herbs, garlic, and cayenne pepper into the buttermilk mixture.

2 Using a large knife, carefully cut each chicken breast half crosswise to make 4 breast portions, for a total of 10 chicken pieces. Add the pieces to the buttermilk brine, making sure that the chicken is submerged. (If it isn't, transfer everything to a smaller bowl.) Cover and refrigerate for at least 4 hours or up to 6 hours.

3 Pour oil to a depth of at least 3 inches (7.5 cm) into a deep, heavy saucepan and warm over high heat to 350°F (180°C) on a deep-frying thermometer. Set a large wire rack on a large rimmed baking sheet and place near the stove. Have ready a second baking sheet. While the oil is heating, in a large bowl, whisk together the flour, baking powder, and ½ teaspoon black pepper. Remove half of the chicken from the buttermilk brine, letting the excess brine drip back into the bowl. Add the chicken to the flour mixture and toss to coat evenly, then transfer to the second baking sheet.

4 When the oil is ready, in batches to avoid crowding, carefully slip the chicken pieces into the hot oil. The temperature will drop, but adjust the heat to keep the oil bubbling steadily at about 325°F (165°C). Deep-fry the chicken pieces, turning them occasionally with tongs, until they are golden brown and show no sign of pink when pierced at the thickest part, about 12 minutes. Using a wire skimmer, transfer the chicken to the rack to drain. Repeat with the remaining chicken. Transfer to a platter, sprinkle with flaky sea salt, and serve right away.

Buttermilk, 4 cups
(32 fl oz/1 l)

Kosher salt and freshly
ground black pepper

Dried thyme, 2 teaspoons

Dried rosemary, 2 teaspoons

Dried sage, 2 teaspoons

Granulated garlic,
1 teaspoon

Cayenne pepper,
½ teaspoon

Cut-up chicken: 2 thighs,
2 drumsticks, 2 wings,
and 2 breast halves
(about 3½ lb/1.75 kg total)

Canola oil, for deep-frying

All-purpose flour, 1⅓ cups
(7 oz/220. g)

Baking powder, 1 teaspoon

Flaky sea salt or kosher salt,
for sprinkling

BRAISE

ALL ABOUT
BRAISING

Braising breaks down tough cuts of meat and dense vegetables into soft, tender morsels by cooking them slowly in a moderate amount of liquid. In many cases, ingredients for braising are first browned to create deep flavor, then the braising liquid, typically a flavored liquid like stock, wine, beer, or tomato sauce, is added. After long, slow cooking, the braising liquid becomes an amazing sauce, with the flavors of all the ingredients mingling together.

To braise means to simmer food slowly in a covered pan in a small amount of liquid. Foods best suited to this long cooking method are tough cuts of meat, poultry, some fish, and many vegetables.

While the process of braising can, at times, take hours to do, it requires very little hands-on time or attention once the ingredients are in the pot. Braised dishes are good choices for entertaining, as their deep flavors will impress your guests and they can often be made ahead of time. Braised foods generally reheat well, too, so it's good to plan on leftovers for a future meal.

Braising can be done in almost any pot that has a tight-fitting lid, as long as the ingredients fit securely once the lid is in place. Use a deep, wide pot, saucepan, or straight-sided sauté pan. If you plan to finish braising in the oven, be sure your chosen pot has a ovenproof handle (i.e., metal, not plastic).

? WHAT'S THE DIFFERENCE BETWEEN BRAISING AND STEWING?

Braising and stewing are very similar cooking methods, and the terms are often used interchangeably. Technically, though, braising refers to large, often whole ingredients, while stewing utilizes smaller pieces. Braised dishes are always made in a covered pot, while stewed dishes aren't necessarily covered. Both use a low and slow cooking method for tender, melt-in-your-mouth results.

WHAT YOU NEED

WIDE, HEAVY POT OR LARGE
STRAIGHT-SIDED SAUTÉ PAN

SET OF RESTAURANT-STYLE TONGS

WOODEN SPOON

FLAVORFUL LIQUID

LOW TO MEDIUM-LOW HEAT

SECRETS TO SUCCESS

PAT FOODS DRY
Soak up the moisture on foods' surface with paper towels before browning. A dry surface will encourage browning.

DON'T CROWD THE FOOD During the browning step, make sure the food sits in the pan in a single layer. Crowded food will steam, rather than brown. Brown in batches, if necessary.

DEGLAZE THE PAN
After browning, add the liquid to the pan and scrape up the browned bits from the pan bottom. These bits are like flavor bombs, adding depth and richness to the finished dish.

SKIM THE SAUCE For the best flavor and texture, take the time to skim the fat off the braising liquid before using it as a sauce.

DO NOT BOIL Adjust the heat periodically to be sure the braising liquid is simmering (small bubbles), not boiling (large bubbles). Boiling could cause the food to toughen up.

{ **VINTAGE BRAISING PANS**

That old Dutch oven that's been handed down in your family for generations is an ideal pan for braising. An enameled cast-iron pan heats up slowly, but holds heat well. It can also be put in the oven for long, slow, hands-off cooking.

HOW TO
BRAISE

1

SEAR THE PROTEIN
Get the pan and oil really hot.
Add the protein, such as brisket
or chicken pieces, and sear well
on all sides. (Many recipes call
for first coating foods with flour.)

2

BROWN STURDY VEGETABLES
Transfer the protein to a plate, then
rewarm the pan for a few seconds.
Add any sturdy vegetables, such as
carrots, onions, and celery, to the pan.

3

DEVELOP THE FLAVOR
Sauté the sturdy vegetables until
they are lightly browned and
slightly softened to help
coax out their flavor.

3

6

4

ADD THE AROMATICS
Add any herbs, spices, and
garlic and sauté them briefly
to bring out their aromas.

5

DEGLAZE
Add broth, wine, or other flavorful
liquid called for in the recipe and
scrape up the delicious browned
bits stuck to the pan bottom. Return
the browned ingredients back to the
pan and proceed with the recipe.

6

SKIM THE SAUCE
Remove the braised ingredients
from the pan and keep warm. Pour
the sauce into a bowl and let stand
for a few minutes. Using a large
spoon, skim the fat from the surface
of the sauce before serving.

BRAISED TUNA
WITH OLIVE RELISH & SPINACH

MAKES 4 SERVINGS

Tuna's mild flavor soaks up braising liquids well, such as this combo of broth, olive oil, and wine. A colorful and piquant olive relish comes together quickly in a food processor, and the orange zest sets it apart from store-bought tapenades. This recipe makes more relish than you need so you'll have leftovers for other meals.

1 In a large sauté pan with a tight-fitting lid, stir together the broth, 4 tablespoons (2 fl oz/60 ml) of the oil, the wine, onion, bay leaves, ½ teaspoon salt, and several grinds of pepper. Bring to a boil over medium-high heat, then reduce the heat to low, cover, and simmer for 30 minutes to blend the flavors.

2 Add the tuna to the pan, re cover, and braise for 15–20 minutes. The tuna should be firm and opaque throughout.

3 In a food processor, combine the olives, garlic, remaining 1 tablespoon oil, the vinegar, and orange zest. Pulse until a chunky texture forms.

4 In a bowl, drizzle the spinach with a little olive oil, season with salt and pepper, and toss to coat evenly. Divide the spinach among individual plates, and then divide the tuna among the plates, arranging it next to or on top of the spinach. Top each tuna portion with a spoonful of the olive relish and serve right away.

{ **PREP WORK: HOW TO PIT OLIVES**
Spread the olives in a single layer on a cutting board. Crush them gently with a rolling pin, the bottom of a pan, or the flat side of a chef's knife. Using your fingers, pull out the pits, using a paring knife to coax out any stubborn ones.

Vegetable broth, ¼ cup (2 fl oz/60 ml)

Extra-virgin olive oil, 5 tablespoons (3 fl oz/ 80 ml), plus more for drizzling

Dry white wine, ¼ cup (2 fl oz/60 ml)

Yellow onion, ½, finely chopped

Bay leaves, 3

Kosher salt and freshly ground pepper

Tuna fillets, 4, about 6 oz (185 g) each

Pitted green olives, 1 cup (5 oz/155 g)

Pitted Kalamata olives, 1 cup (5 oz/155 g)

Garlic, 2 cloves chopped

Red wine vinegar, 1 teaspoon

Orange zest, grated from 1 orange

Baby spinach, 4 cups (4 oz/125 g)

GARLIC CHICKEN

MAKES 4-6 SERVINGS

Garlic lovers rejoice! Four whole heads of garlic might sound excessive, but as it cooks, the garlic mellows and turns sweet and nutty, adding depth to the pan juices that are served over the chicken. The pulp of the cooked garlic helps thicken the sauce, but it's fun leave a few cloves whole for squeezing onto crusty bread at the table.

1 Season the chicken all over with salt and pepper. In a large pot with a tight-fitting lid over medium-high heat, warm the oil. Working in batches, add the chicken and cook, turning frequently, until well browned, 7–10 minutes. Transfer to a plate.

2 Pour off all but 2 tablespoons of the fat in the pan. Add the garlic cloves and sauté over medium-high heat until lightly browned, about 3 minutes. Pour in the wine and stir to scrape up the browned bits on the bottom of the pan with a wooden spoon. Sprinkle with the thyme. Return the chicken to the pot. Bring the liquid just to a boil, then immediately reduce the heat to low, cover, and braise until the chicken is tender and opaque throughout, about 45 minutes.

3 Uncover the pot and check one of the thickest chicken pieces; the meat should be cooked through and falling off the bone. If not, re-cover and continue cooking, checking again for doneness every 10 or 15 minutes.

4 Transfer the chicken to a platter and cover loosely with foil to keep warm. Set aside a few garlic cloves. Set a fine-mesh sieve over a saucepan and strain the pan juices through the sieve into the pan. Press on the garlic cloves to extract as much liquid and pulp as possible. Bring to a simmer over medium-high heat and season to taste with salt and pepper.

5 Transfer the chicken to a platter and pour the cooking liquid over the top. Serve the chicken right away with the bread and reserved garlic cloves for squeezing.

Cut-up chicken: 2 thighs, 2 drumsticks, 2 wings, and 2 breast halves (about 3½ lb/1.75 kg total)

Kosher salt and freshly ground pepper

Canola oil, 2 tablespoons

Garlic, 4 heads, separated into cloves, unpeeled

Dry white wine, ¾ cup (6 fl oz/375 ml)

Fresh thyme, 1 tablespoon chopped

Hot crusty bread, for serving

MEXICAN POT ROAST

MAKES 8 SERVINGS

Here, we took the classic concept of slow-braised, fork-tender, simmered-in-spices pot roast and added even more goodness in the form of Mexican flavors. The meat is braised in a zesty sauce of tomatillos and chipotles, then it's served with dense hominy. Avocado and cilantro garnishes complete the south-of-the-border theme.

1 Preheat the oven to 300°F (150°C). Place the roast in a large bowl, season generously with salt and pepper, and dust with the flour.

2 Warm a large ovenproof pot with a tight fitting lid over medium heat, and add 2 tablespoons of the oil. Add the roast and cook until browned all over, about 12 minutes. Transfer to a plate. Add the onion and garlic to the pot and sauté until softened, about 5 minutes. Add the broth, bay leaves, tomatillos, and chipotles and bring to a boil, stirring to scrape up the browned bits on the pan bottom. Return the roast to the pot, cover, and place in oven. Set the timer for 1½ hours.

3 Remove the pot from the oven. Uncover, and using long-handled tongs, turn over the meat. Re-cover, put the pot back in the oven, and braise for 1¼ hours more. During the last 30 minutes of braising, add the hominy to the pot.

4 Transfer the roast to a cutting board and remove the strings. Cut the roast across the grain into thick slices and arrange on a platter along with the vegetables. Spoon the cooking liquid and hominy on top. Serve the sour cream, green onions, avocados, and cilantro on the side for guests to add as desired.

{ INGREDIENT DEMYSTIFIED: TOMATILLOS
Tomatillos—the key ingredient in famed salsa verde—have a lemony, herbal flavor. They look like little, sturdy green tomatoes, and grow in a papery husk. Before using, peel off the husks, then rinse the tomatillos under warm running water to rid them of their sticky, resinous coating.

Chuck roast, 4 lb (2 kg), tied

Kosher salt and freshly ground pepper

All-purpose flour, ¼ cup (1½ oz/45 g)

Olive oil, 6 tablespoons (3 fl oz/90 ml)

Yellow onion, 1, cut into 8 pieces

Garlic, 6 cloves, crushed

Beef broth, 5 cups (40 fl oz/1.25 l)

Bay leaves, 2

Tomatillos, 6, husked and rinsed

Canned chipotle chiles in adobo sauce, 4, chopped

Canned hominy, 3 cups (20 oz/625 g), drained

Sour cream, 1 cup (8 oz/250 g)

Green onions, 1 cup (3 oz/90 g) thinly sliced

Avocados, 2, pitted, peeled, and diced

Fresh cilantro, 2 tablespoons torn leaves

STOUT-BRAISED CHICKEN

MAKES 4-6 SERVINGS

Here, chicken, potatoes, and vegetables are braised until fork-tender in a rich sauce of stout and garlic. That's right, beer-cooked chicken. The stout lends a deep, roasted essence, while the garlic intensifies the broth with homey flavors. Enjoy this meal with an extra bottle of your favorite stout served alongside.

1 Season the chicken all over with salt and pepper. In a large pot with a tight-fitting lid over medium-high heat, warm the oil. Working in batches if necessary, add the chicken and cook, turning frequently, until well browned, 7 10 minutes. Transfer to a plate.

2 Pour off all but 2 tablespoons fat from the pot. Add the onions and garlic and sauté until lightly browned, about 3 minutes. Add the potatoes, carrots, and cabbage to the pot. Return the chicken to the pot. Pour in the stout and stir to combine the ingredients. Bring to a boil over medium-high heat, then reduce the heat to low, and simmer until the chicken is falling-off-the-bone-tender, about 45 minutes.

3 Uncover the pot and check one of the thickest chicken pieces; the meat should be cooked through and falling off the bone. If not, re-cover and continue cooking, checking again for doneness every 10 or 15 minutes.

4 Using a slotted spoon, transfer the chicken and vegetables to a platter, or divide among large, shallow individual bowls. Using a large spoon, skim any fat from the surface of the cooking liquid and discard Squeeze the cooked garlic cloves from their skins into the pot and stir until the garlic is mixed into the liquid. Spoon the cooking liquid over the chicken.

5 Put dollops of sour cream around the platter or on each serving. Garnish with parsley and serve right away.

Cut-up chicken: 2 thighs, 2 drumsticks, 2 wings, and 2 breast halves (about 3½ lb/1.75 kg total)

Kosher salt and freshly ground pepper

Canola oil, 2 tablespoons

Yellow onions, 1 lb (500 g), quartered

Garlic, 5 cloves, unpeeled

Red potatoes, 1 lb (500 g), scrubbed and cut into ½-inch (12-mm) chunks

Carrots, 1 lb (500 g), peeled and chopped

Green cabbage, ½ small head, trimmed, cored and chopped

Stout, 1 bottle (12 fl oz/375 ml)

Sour cream, ¼ cup (2 oz/60 g)

Fresh flat-leaf parsley, chopped, for garnish

CARNITAS TACOS

Carnitas, literally "little meats" in Spanish, is pork that's often shredded and used as a taco filling. Traditionally, the meat simmers in its own fat, but here we used tangy citrus juices and beer for a lighter and zestier version. This recipe yields a lot of meat, so call up your friends, blend some margaritas, and make a party out of it.

1 Preheat the oven to 350°F (180°C). In a small bowl, combine 2 teaspoons salt and 1 teaspoon pepper. Season the pork generously with the mixture. Set aside.

2 In a large ovenproof pot with a tight-fitting lid over medium-high heat, warm the oil. Add the pork, and cook, turning frequently until browned on all sides, about 10 minutes. Transfer to a plate.

3 Pour off all but a thin layer of fat in the pan. Add the onion and garlic and sauté until they begin to soften, 1–2 minutes. Pour in the beer and stir to scrape up the browned bits on the bottom of the pan with a wooden spoon. Return the pork to the pot. Add the orange and lime zests and juices and the oregano. Cover, then put the pot in the oven and set the timer for 1½ hours.

4 Remove the pot from the oven. Uncover, and using long-handled tongs, turn over the meat. Re-cover, put the pot back in the oven, and braise until the pork is very tender, 1¼ hours more.

5 Transfer the pork to a cutting board and cover loosely with aluminum foil to keep warm. Using a large, shallow spoon or a ladle, skim as much fat as possible from the surface of the cooking liquid. Using a large, sharp knife and a fork, coarsely cut and shred the pork into small bite-sized pieces. Arrange the meat on a platter or individual plates, moisten it lightly with the cooking juices, and serve right away with the tortillas, lime wedges, onion, salsa, and cilantro. Let diners assemble their own tacos.

Kosher salt and freshly ground pepper

Boneless pork shoulder roast, 3–4 lb (1.5–2 kg)

Olive oil, ¼ cup (2 fl oz/60 ml)

Yellow onion, 1, finely chopped

Garlic, 2 cloves, minced

Mexican lager-style beer, 1 bottle (12 fl oz/375 ml)

Large orange, 1, grated zest and juice

Lime, 1, grated zest and juice

Dried oregano, 1 tablespoon

Warm corn or flour tortillas, lime wedges, chopped white onion, hot or mild salsa, and chopped fresh cilantro, for serving

BEEF BRAISED IN RED WINE

MAKES 6 SERVINGS

Like many braised dishes, this dish is better when made 1 or 2 days in advance;
make it on the weekend when you know you have a busy week ahead and rewarm
the meat and sauce gently over medium-low heat. Serve it with polenta
(see page 105) or mashed potatoes (see page 107) for soaking up the juices.

1 Preheat the oven to 300°F (150°C). In a small bowl, stir together the parsley, rosemary, sage, and garlic. Set aside. On a large plate, stir together the flour, paprika, 1 teaspoon salt, and ½ teaspoon pepper. Dredge the brisket in the flour mixture, shaking off the excess.

2 In a large ovenproof pot with a tight-fitting lid over medium-high heat, warm 2 tablespoons of the oil. Add the brisket and cook until browned on all sides, about 10 minutes. Transfer to a plate. Add the remaining 1 tablespoon oil to the pot, then add the bacon and sauté until the fat is rendered, about 5 minutes. Add the onion and sauté until softened, 3–4 minutes. Add carrots and celery and sauté until slightly softened, about 5 minutes. Add the garlic-herb mixture and bay leaves and stir well until aromatic, about 1 minute.

3 Add 1 cup (8 fl oz/250 ml) of the wine to the pot and bring to a boil, stirring to scrape up the browned bits on the pan bottom. Let the mixture boil until the liquid is reduced by half. Add the remaining 2 cups (16 fl oz/500 ml) wine and season lightly with salt and pepper. Bring the liquid to a simmer, then return the brisket to the pot. Cover, place in the oven, and cook until the brisket is fork-tender, 4–5 hours. Turn the brisket over in the pan every hour to ensure even cooking.

4 Transfer the brisket to a cutting board. Carefully pour the contents of the pan through a fine-mesh sieve into a bowl. Discard the solids in the sieve and let the liquid stand for a few minutes while you cut the brisket across the grain into thick slices. Using a large spoon, skim the fat from the surface of the liquid. Taste the liquid and adjust the seasoning if necessary. Transfer the meat to a platter, pour over the liquid, and serve right away.

Fresh flat-leaf parsley,
3 tablespoons minced

Fresh rosemary,
2 tablespoons minced

Fresh sage, 2 teaspoons
minced

Garlic, 4 cloves, minced

All-purpose flour, ⅓ cup
(2 oz/60 g)

Paprika, 1 teaspoon

Kosher salt and freshly
ground pepper

Flat-cut beef brisket, 3 lb
(1.5 kg), excess fat trimmed

Olive oil, 3 tablespoons

Smoked bacon, 3 slices,
cut crosswise into strips
¼ inch (6 mm) wide

Small yellow onion, 1,
thinly sliced

Carrots, 2, peeled and diced

Celery, 2 stalks, diced

Bay leaves, 2

Dry red wine, such as
Syrah or Shiraz, 3 cups
(24 fl oz/750 ml)

COLLARD GREENS, SOUTHERN-STYLE

MAKES 4-6 SERVINGS

Regardless of where you grew up, it's hard not to appreciate home-style
southern cooking. These collards meet all the southern standards: versatile,
comforting, easy to prepare, and they include bacon. For the best flavor,
buy the bacon in a big slab from the butcher and dice it at home.

1 Remove the coarse stems and center ribs from the collard greens,
then rinse and drain the leaves. Spin the leaves completely dry
and then coarsely chop.

2 In a small frying pan over medium-high heat, sauté the bacon until
browned, about 6 minutes. Transfer to a paper towel–lined plate
and set aside.

3 In a large pot with a tight-fitting lid, bring the water to a boil. Add
the greens to the pot, reduce the heat to medium-high, cover partially,
and braise, stirring occasionally, until very tender, about 45 minutes.

4 If any liquid remains, drain the greens before transferring them to
a serving bowl. Season with black pepper. Stir in the bacon and red
pepper flakes. Serve warm, passing the pepper vinegar at the table.

Collard greens, 5½ lb (2.75 kg)

Smoked bacon, ¼ lb (125 g), finely diced

Water, 4 qt (4 l)

Freshly ground black pepper

Red pepper flakes, ½ teaspoon

Pepper-infused vinegar, for serving

{ BUYING GREENS FOR COOKING
When shopping for greens that will later be cooked—such as
spinach, kale, collards, etc.—buy more greens then you think
you need. Trust us. Because greens have a high water density,
they cook down significantly under heat and will shrink down
to next to nothing. Plan on buying at least 1 pound (500 g)
of fresh greens per person.

RED WINE-BRAISED RED CABBAGE & APPLES

This dish begs to be eaten in chilly weather with roasted poultry or meat—pork is a particularly good partner. Cabbage and apples make a colorful, healthful, and pleasantly tart duo. Here, they're braised in bacon fat, sugar, thyme, and vinegar to create a meltingly tender texture and smoky, sweet-sour flavor.

1 Cut the cabbage in half lengthwise and remove the core. Cut the cabbage into slices ½ inch (12 mm) thick. Set aside.

2 In a large pot with a tight-fitting lid over medium-high heat, sauté the bacon until lightly browned, about 5 minutes. Transfer to a paper towel-lined plate and set aside.

3 Pour off all but 1 tablespoon of the fat in the pan. Add the onion and sauté over medium-high heat until slightly softened, about 3 minutes. Stir in the apples, vinegar, brown sugar, and thyme, raise the heat to high, and stir to scrape up the browned bits on the bottom of the pan with a wooden spoon.

4 Add the cabbage to the pot, season with salt and pepper, and stir to combine. Cover and braise until tender, about 30 minutes. Stir in the reserved bacon and serve right away.

Red cabbage, 1 large head, about 3 lb (1.5 kg), bruised or discolored outer leaves removed

Smoked bacon, 6 slices, chopped

Red onion, 1, thinly sliced

Granny Smith apples, 2, peeled, cored, and cut into ½-inch (12-mm) cubes

Red wine vinegar, ⅓ cup (3 fl oz/80 ml)

Light brown sugar, 2 tablespoons firmly packed

Fresh thyme, 2 teaspoons chopped

Kosher salt and freshly ground pepper

SHORT RIB RAGÙ

This sauce is a game changer: it's so easy to make, yet it's so impressive, your friends will think you've seriously upped your cooking game when they eat it. Serve it over wide pasta ribbons or creamy mashed potatoes (page 107). It takes a few hours to cook, but once everything's in the pot, you can pretty much leave it alone.

1 Trim the short ribs of excess fat. Thoroughly pat the meat dry with paper towels.

2 In a large, heavy pot with a tight-fitting lid over medium-high heat, warm 1 tablespoon of the oil. Add the prosciutto and sauté until lightly browned, 2–3 minutes. Using a slotted spoon, transfer the prosciutto to a large platter and set aside. Working in batches, add the short ribs to the pot and brown on all sides, about 12 minutes. Transfer the beef and its juices to the platter.

3 Add the remaining 2 tablespoons oil to the pot and stir in the onion, carrot, garlic, bay leaves, cinnamon, and cumin. Sauté until the vegetables are softened, lightly colored, and aromatic, about 10 minutes. Return the short ribs and prosciutto to the pot, add 1 teaspoon salt and several grinds of pepper, and stir well. Stir in the tomato paste, wine, and enough broth just to cover the meat. Cover partially, reduce the heat to low, and braise, stirring occasionally, until the meat is tender, about 3 hours.

4 Remove the pot from the heat and remove and discard the bay leaves. Carefully pour the contents of the pan through a fine-mesh sieve into a bowl. Transfer the short ribs to a cutting board. Using your hands or 2 forks, shred the meat into bite-sized pieces. Return the meat to the pot. Let the liquid stand for a few minutes. Using a large spoon, skim the fat from the surface of the liquid. Taste the liquid and adjust the seasoning if necessary. Pour the liquid over the meat in the pan and rewarm over medium-low heat before serving.

Bone-in beef short ribs, 4 lb (2 kg)

Olive oil, 3 tablespoons

Prosciutto, 2 oz (60 g), cut into narrow strips

Large yellow onion, 1, chopped

Carrot, 1, peeled and chopped

Garlic, 1 large clove, minced

Bay leaves, 2

Cinnamon stick

Ground cumin, 1 teaspoon

Kosher salt and freshly ground pepper

Tomato paste, 3 tablespoons

Dry red wine, ½ cup (4 fl oz/125 ml)

Beef broth, 3½ cups (28 fl oz/875 ml), or as needed

BRAISED BROCCOLI RABE *&* OLIVES

MAKES 4 SERVINGS

Braised with garlic, olives, anchovies, and wine–this is broccoli rabe like you've never had it before. It's a versatile side dish for sausages, roast chicken, or pork chops, or you can toss it with cooked pasta or use it as a topping on bruschetta.

1 Bring a large saucepan of water to a boil over high heat. Add the broccoli rabe and cook just until wilted, 3–4 minutes. Drain and let cool for 5 minutes, then chop very coarsely.

2 In a large frying pan with a tight-fitting lid over medium-low heat, warm the garlic in the olive oil, stirring often, until the garlic is softened but not browned, about 7 minutes. Stir in the olives, anchovies, if using, and pepper flakes and sauté until fragrant, about 1 minute.

3 Raise the heat to medium and add the broccoli rabe to the pan, stirring to combine. Pour in the wine, raise the heat to medium-high, and bring to a simmer. Reduce the heat to medium-low, cover partially, and braise until the broccoli rabe is tender and most of the liquid has been absorbed, 15–20 minutes. Season with salt, if needed, and serve right away.

Broccoli rabe, 1¼ lb (625 g), tough stems removed

Garlic, 2 large cloves, minced

Olive oil, 3 tablespoons

Pitted Kalamata olives, ½ cup (2½ oz/75 g), sliced

Italian oil-packed anchovy fillets, 1–2, finely chopped (optional)

Red pepper flakes, generous pinch

Dry white wine, 1 cup (8 fl oz/250 ml)

Kosher salt

{ INGREDIENT DEMYSTIFIED:
BROCCOLI RABE Broccoli rabe is like broccoli's older, cooler cousin. The two vegetables come from the same cruciferous family, but broccoli rabe is a bit stalkier and has more leaves. It also has a slightly more bitter taste and crunchier stalk. A bit of acid in the preparation (wine, vinegar, lemon juice) helps counter the bitter taste of the vegetable, but if you or your guests don't like bitter vegetables (it's a love-hate thing), you can substitute baby broccoli in most recipes.

SIMMER & POACH

ALL ABOUT
SIMMERING
& POACHING

Simmering and poaching are similar cooking techniques. You can distinguish each method by the size of the bubbles and the frequency with which they break the surface of a heated liquid: Simmering calls for consistent, medium-to-small bubbles, while poaching demands very small, infrequent bubbles.

The ingredient being cooked usually dictates which technique to use: simmering works for a wide variety of vegetables, grains, legumes, sauces, custards, and stove-top puddings. Poaching is best for very delicate foods that can easily overcook, such as fish, shellfish, white-meat poultry, eggs, and fruit.

Simmering and poaching are moist-heat cooking techniques that gently cook foods to tenderness in a hot liquid. Both methods help retain the color and texture of the raw ingredient.

You don't need special cookware for simmering. Any saucepan or sauté pan will do, although if you intend to reduce a volume of liquid, a pan with a wide base and large surface area will help the process go faster. For poaching, choose a pan that is not much larger than the food to be poached, but that still allows the cooking liquid to flow easily around the food. You don't need to hunt for a matching lid for your cookware, as simmering and poaching are both done uncovered.

HOW DO YOU BOIL WATER, REALLY?

No one really ever teaches you how to boil water, but there actually is a right way. It's a useful thing to know because many recipes call for bringing liquids to a boil first, then reducing the heat to create the desired size and frequency of bubbles in the liquid. So here you have it, once and for all: the right way to boil water

1 Start with cold (not hot) water from the tap and add it to a pan.

2 Set the pan over medium-high to high heat.

3 Wait (don't watch) for the water to boil. The timing will depend on your elevation. Covering the pan is optional, but it can make things go quicker.

STRAIGHT-SIDED SAUTÉ PAN
OR SAUCEPAN

SECRETS TO SUCCESS

ADJUST THE HEAT
When simmering or poaching foods, check the pot from time to time to make sure the bubbles stay at the intended size. Adjust the heat up or down as necessary.

TEST FOR TASTE
The flavors of simmering ingredients will develop as they cook. Taste and adjust the seasonings toward the end of the cooking time.

POACHING ASSURANCE
If you're uncertain of how the liquid should look when poaching, use an instant-read thermometer to check the liquid. An ideal poaching temperature is between 160° and 180°F (71° and 82°C).

TIMING IS EVERYTHING When poaching, be sure to remove the food from the liquid as soon as it is done to prevent it from overcooking.

WHISK

SLOTTED SPOON OR
WOODEN SPOON

SIMMERING TO REDUCE

No, it's not a new way to lose weight, rather it's a way to make simmered dishes taste even more delicious. Reducing means to simmer a liquid with the goal of decreasing its volume through the process of evaporation. Reducing also concentrates flavors and thickens the liquid's consistency. Be careful when reducing salty liquids, as the saltiness will only intensify as it cooks down.

COLANDER

LOW TO MEDIUM HEAT

HOW TO
SIMMER

1
CHECK FREQUENTLY
Be sure that the bubbles in the
liquid are small to medium in size,
adjusting the heat if necessary.
Push the food aside to monitor
the level of reducing liquids.

2
TEST FOR DONENESS
Test simmered meats and
vegetables by tasting a bite.
Test the texture of custards
by dragging a finger across
them on a spoon.

1
BOIL WATER
Bring the liquid to a boil, then reduce the heat so that small bubbles occasionally break the surface of the liquid. Ease in the food to be cooked.

HOW TO
POACH

2
LIFT & SEPARATE
Use a slotted spoon to nudge the food in the pan so that the liquid flows evenly around the pieces. Remove the food as soon as it's done.

3
BLOT DRY
Briefly blot the food on a paper towel before serving to remove excess liquid.

EGGS BENNY

Eggs Benedict is a quintessential brunch item. It's easy to see why: crispy toasted English muffins are piled with thinly sliced, salty ham, topped with a plump, poached egg, and drizzled with lemony hollandaise sauce. Our take features prosciutto and hollandaise made in a blender, making the whole process all the more simple.

1 To make the hollandaise sauce, in a blender, combine the egg yolks, 1 tablespoon water, the lemon juice, ¼ teaspoon salt, and the cayenne. In a small saucepan over medium heat, melt the butter. With the blender running, slowly add the warm melted butter through the vent in the lid, processing until the sauce is thick and smooth. Taste and adjust the seasoning. If the sauce is too thick, add a bit more water to thin it. Transfer to a bowl, cover, and set aside.

2 Pour water to a depth of 3 inches (7.5 cm) into a large sauté pan, add a pinch of salt, and bring to a simmer over medium heat. Working with 4 eggs at a time, crack each egg into a small ramekin, removing any shells and starting anew if any yolks break. Carefully ease the eggs into the water. Adjust the heat so that the water barely simmers. Poach the eggs for 3–5 minutes, then remove from the water with a slotted spoon. Lightly blot the eggs on a paper towel–lined plate to drain, then transfer to a dish and keep warm. Repeat to poach the remaining 4 eggs.

3 Place 2 English muffin halves, cut side up, on each of 4 individual plates. Lay a prosciutto slice on each muffin half. Top the prosciutto with a poached egg, and spoon some warm hollandaise sauce over each egg. Grind some black pepper over the top and serve right away.

FOR THE HOLLANDAISE SAUCE

Large egg yolks, 4, at room temperature

Water, 1 tablespoon, plus more as needed

Fresh lemon juice, 1 tablespoon

Kosher salt, ¼ teaspoon

Cayenne pepper, small pinch

Unsalted butter, 1 cup (8 oz/250 g)

Kosher salt and freshly ground black pepper

Large eggs, 8

English muffins, 4, split and toasted

Prosciutto, 8 slices, at room temperature

CREAMY POLENTA & VEGETABLE RAGOUT

MAKES 4 SERVINGS

This sophisticated meal is easy to prepare and leftovers taste great even a few days after cooking. Polenta is a corn-based whole grain that simmers into a naturally creamy porridge. It's similar to grits, but has a smoother consistency that makes a delicious base for hearty vegetable ragout.

1 In a frying pan over medium heat, warm 2 tablespoons of the oil. Add the onion and sauté until soft, about 4 minutes. Add the garlic, zucchini, and mushrooms and sauté, stirring occasionally, until the vegetables are soft, 4–5 minutes. Add the tomatoes, rosemary, sherry, ½ teaspoon salt, and a few grinds of pepper. Continue to simmer, stirring often, until the tomatoes release their juices and are softened, 3–4 minutes.

2 Meanwhile, in a saucepan over high heat, bring the broth to a boil. Whisk in the polenta and ½ teaspoon salt. Reduce the heat to low and simmer, stirring often, until the polenta is thick and creamy, 25–30 minutes. Remove from the heat and stir in the remaining 1 tablespoon oil and the cheese.

3 Spoon the polenta into shallow individual bowls, top with the ragout, and serve right away.

{ FANCY FOOD TERM: RAGOUT   Ragout is a French word that roughly means stew. A ragout (pronounced "rag-GOO") can be made from all sorts of meats, vegetables, and sometimes even fruit. The nice thing about a ragout is you don't have to feel limited to the ingredients listed in the recipe. As long as they have a similar texture and cooking time, vegetables can be replaced with your favorite choices, and mixed and matched for endless variations.

Olive oil, 3 tablespoons

Yellow onion, 1, chopped

Garlic, 2 small cloves, minced

Zucchini, 1, sliced

Cremini mushrooms, 1 lb (500 g), sliced

Ripe plum tomatoes, ½ lb (250 g), chopped

Fresh rosemary, 2 teaspoons minced

Dry sherry, ¼ cup (2 fl oz/60 ml)

Kosher salt and freshly ground pepper

Vegetable or chicken broth, 4 cups (32 fl oz/1 l)

Polenta, 1 cup (7 oz/220 g)

Parmesan cheese, ¼ cup (1 oz/30 g) freshly grated

PENNE AL'ARRABBIATA

This is a great dish to whip up for a hungry crowd, without needing to spend a lot of time or money. The sauce gets its name from the Italian word arrabbiata, which means "angry." Here, it refers to the kick of spice provided by red pepper flakes. You can always add less or more pepper flakes, depending on your spice preference.

1 In a large frying pan over medium heat, warm the oil. Add the pancetta and cook, stirring often, until browned, 2–3 minutes. Add the onion, garlic, and red pepper flakes and sauté until the onion is softened and translucent, 3–5 minutes. Stir in the tomatoes with their juice and ½ teaspoon salt, using a fork to crush and break up the tomatoes. Simmer, uncovered, until the sauce has thickened slightly, 10–15 minutes. Remove from the heat and keep warm.

2 Meanwhile, bring a large pot of salted water to a boil. Add the pasta, stir, and simmer, stirring occasionally, until al dente, according to the package directions. Drain the pasta.

3 Transfer the drained pasta to the pan with the sauce, place over low heat, and toss briefly to coat thoroughly. Add half of the cheese and toss to mix evenly. Transfer to a warmed serving bowl, sprinkle with the parsley, and serve right away. Pass the remaining cheese at the table.

Olive oil, 1 tablespoon

Pancetta, 3 oz (90 g), diced

Yellow onion, 1, finely chopped

Garlic, 2 cloves, minced

Red pepper flakes, ¾ teaspoon, or to taste

Whole plum tomatoes, 1 can (28 oz/875 g)

Kosher salt

Penne pasta, 1 lb (500 g)

Pecorino romano cheese, ½ cup (2 oz/60 g), freshly grated

Fresh flat-leaf parsley, ¼ cup (⅓ oz/10 g) chopped

{ **INGREDIENT DEMYSTIFIED: PANCETTA**
Pancetta is an Italian version of bacon, but, like most bacon, it's not smoked. Pancetta is made from pork belly that has been rubbed with salt and spices, such as cinnamon, cloves, juniper, and black pepper, then rolled into a tight cylinder to be cured for at least two months. You can find pancetta sliced or diced next to the bacon in some grocery stores, or in upscale delis and butcher shops.

SOUR CREAM MASHED POTATOES

There's nothing quite as satisfying as creamy, homemade mashed potatoes.
Here, the creaminess is emphasized by mashing the potatoes with a mixture of milk,
sour cream, and butter for a silky richness. The sour cream lends a slight tartness
that's reminiscent of mashed potatoes served in diners and at Grandma's house.

1 Peel and quarter the potatoes. Fill a saucepan about three-fourths full of water, add 2 tablespoons salt, and then the potatoes and garlic, if using. Bring to a boil, reduce the heat to low, and simmer, uncovered, until the potatoes are tender when pierced with the tip of a paring knife, about 30 minutes. Drain the potatoes.

2 Place the potatoes in a large bowl and use a potato masher or a large fork to mash them to the desired texture. Cover the bowl with a kitchen towel to keep warm.

3 In a small saucepan over medium heat, combine the milk, sour cream, and butter, and bring to just below a boil. Immediately remove from the heat. Gradually add the milk mixture to the potatoes while stirring with a fork. The potatoes should be smooth and thick. Beat the potatoes a few times with a large spoon to smooth them out. Season with salt, and serve right away.

Yukon gold potatoes, 4 large, about 2 lb (1 kg) total weight

Kosher salt

Garlic, 3 large cloves (optional)

Whole milk, ½ cup (4 fl oz/125 ml)

Sour cream, ½ cup (4 oz/125 g)

Unsalted butter, 2 tablespoons

MOROCCAN-STYLE LAMB STEW

Stews, like this exotically spiced version, are easy when you have the right ingredients and tools on hand. Brown the meat in a pot large enough that the meat isn't crowded, then add the aromatics and let it simmer until fork-tender. Cook some pearl couscous according to the package directions and serve it alongside.

1 In a small saucepan, warm the broth over medium-low heat. Crumble in the saffron. Remove from the heat and set aside.

2 Season the lamb chunks generously with salt and pepper. In a large, heavy pot, warm the oil over medium-high heat. When the oil is shimmering, add the lamb and brown on all sides, about 5 minutes total. With a slotted spoon, transfer to a platter.

3 Add the onion to the pot and sauté until softened, about 5 minutes. Stir in the ginger, paprika, cumin, and garlic and stir for 1 minute. Return the lamb to the pot and add the saffron broth, bay leaf, lemon zest, and ½ teaspoon salt. Season with pepper. Cook over the lowest possible heat—so the liquid barely simmers—until the lamb is tender, at least 1½ hours. Check occasionally; if the liquid level falls too low, add 1 or 2 tablespoons water.

4 Transfer the lamb to a platter and tent loosely with foil. Discard the bay leaf from the braising juices and, if desired, tip the pot and spoon off some of the fat. Add the olives and simmer briskly over medium-high heat until the juices are reduced and concentrated, about 5 minutes. Return the lamb to the pot and season to taste with salt and pepper.

5 Spoon the stew into individual bowls. Sprinkle with parsley, if desired, and serve right away.

Chicken broth, 1½ cups (12 fl oz/375 ml)

Saffron threads, ½ teaspoon

Lamb stew meat, 2 lb (1 kg)

Kosher salt and freshly ground pepper

Olive oil, 2 tablespoons

Yellow onion, 1, finely chopped

Ground ginger, 1 teaspoon

Sweet paprika, ½ teaspoon

Ground cumin, ½ teaspoon

Garlic, 2 cloves, minced

Bay leaf, 1

Lemon, ½, zest removed with a vegetable peeler and chopped

Water, 1–2 tablespoons (optional)

Green olives, 12

Fresh flat-leaf parsley, 2 tablespoons chopped (optional)

BITTER GREENS SALAD
WITH BACON & POACHED EGGS

This simple salad is often served in chic cafes for upwards of $10 a plate. Luckily, you can make it at home in just a few easy steps. Wash some frisée; whisk up a quick vinaigrette; sauté some bacon; and poach a few eggs. Combine everything together, and lunch is served.

1 Tear the frisée into bite-sized pieces, if desired, and put it in a large bowl. In a small bowl, combine the shallot with the vinegar, ½ teaspoon salt, and a few grindings of pepper. Let stand for 10 minutes. Whisk in the oil to make a vinaigrette. Taste and adjust the seasoning with salt and pepper.

2 Put the bacon in a sauté pan over medium heat and fry until crisp, about 5 minutes. Transfer the bacon pieces to the bowl with the frisée. Add the vinaigrette to the bowl and toss the salad to combine all the ingredients. Taste and add a pinch of salt, if necessary. Divide the salad among individual plates.

3 Pour water to a depth of 3 inches (7.5 cm) into a large sauté pan, add a pinch of salt, and bring to a simmer over medium heat. Crack each egg into a small ramekin, removing any shells and starting anew if any yolks break. Carefully ease the eggs into the water. Adjust the heat so that the water barely simmers. Poach the eggs for 3–5 minutes.

4 Remove each egg from the water with a slotted spoon, and while the egg is still in the spoon, blot the bottom dry with a kitchen towel. Gently place an egg on each salad and serve right away.

Frisée, 2 heads, leaves separated

Small shallot, 1, minced

Sherry vinegar, 2 tablespoons

Kosher salt and freshly ground pepper

Olive oil, ½ cup (4 fl oz/125 ml)

Smoked bacon, 4 thick slices, cut crosswise into ½-inch (12-mm) pieces

Large eggs, 4

GREEN BEANS & PANCETTA VINAIGRETTE

Served as a side to roasted meat, eaten straight from the pan, or just enjoyed as cold leftovers, you can't go wrong with this dish. Green beans are simmered until just tender, retaining their crisp bite and green color, then coated in a salty-sour pancetta vinaigrette. If you prefer, the pancetta can be replaced with bacon.

1 In a frying pan over medium-high heat, fry the pancetta until crisp, about 5 minutes. Transfer to a paper towel–lined plate to drain. Pour off all but 1 tablespoon of the fat from the pan.

2 Return the pan to medium heat. Add the onion and sauté until softened, 1–2 minutes. Transfer to a small bowl and whisk in 2 tablespoons of the olive oil, the vinegar, mustard, salt to taste, and 1 teaspoon pepper to make a vinaigrette. Wipe out the pan.

3 Bring a pot full of salted water to a boil over high heat. Add the green beans, reduce the heat to medium, and simmer until the beans are just tender, 5–7 minutes. Drain, rinse under running cold water, and wrap in a kitchen towel to dry. (This process is sometimes referred to as blanching—see Note below.)

4 Warm the frying pan over medium-high heat, and add the remaining 2 tablespoons oil. When the oil is hot, add the green beans and sauté until hot, 3–4 minutes. Remove from the heat and stir in the vinaigrette. Transfer to a bowl, top with the pancetta, and serve.

Pancetta, 4 oz (125 g), diced

Red onion, 3 tablespoons, finely chopped

Olive oil, 4 tablespoons (2 fl oz/60 ml)

Red wine vinegar, 1½ tablespoons

Dijon mustard, ½ teaspoon

Kosher salt and freshly ground pepper

Green beans, 2 lb (1 kg), trimmed

{ **FANCY FOOD TERM: BLANCHING**
Blanching helps retain the crispness and color of a vegetable, while softening it slightly. Food is submerged in a generous amount of rapidly simmering water for a few seconds or for up to a minute or two, then it's immediately drained and plunged into very cold or ice water to stop the cooking process and lock in a bright color. Blanching also works as an aid for removing tough peels from tomatoes and peaches.

CREAMY RISOTTO

This surprisingly easy risotto (the hardest part about this recipe is practicing patience while it simmers) is delicious on its own, but is also a great neutral base for experimenting with different flavors. Try mixing and matching your favorite vegetables, herbs, and grated cheeses—colorful add-ons really enhance the dish.

1 In a small saucepan, combine the broth and water and bring to a gentle simmer over medium heat. Reduce the heat to the lowest setting to keep the broth at a bare simmer.

2 Heat a large saucepan over medium heat and add the butter. When the butter has melted, add the onion and sauté until translucent, about 4 minutes. Season with salt and pepper.

3 Add the rice and sauté until the grains are coated with butter and are hot and translucent, about 3 minutes. Add the wine, bring to a boil, and stir briskly until the wine is absorbed. Add a small ladleful of the hot broth and stir until almost completely absorbed. Continue to add the hot broth, a small ladleful at a time, cooking and stirring until the broth is nearly absorbed before adding more.

4 The rice is ready when the grains are almost tender to the bite but still slightly firm at the center. This will take about 18 minutes from when you first added the broth. If the rice is not ready, add more broth and cook for a few minutes longer.

5 Stir in the cheese and season to taste with salt and pepper. Serve right away.

Chicken broth, 3 cups (24 fl oz/750 ml)

Water, 2 cups (16 fl oz/500 ml)

Unsalted butter, 2 tablespoons

Yellow onion, ½ cup (2½ oz/75 g) finely chopped

Kosher salt and freshly ground pepper

Arborio rice, 1 cup (7 oz/220 g)

Dry white wine, 1 cup (8 fl oz/250 ml)

Parmesan cheese, ¼ cup (1 oz/30 g) freshly grated

{ INGREDIENT DEMYSTIFIED:
ARBORIO RICE   You can't just use any kind of rice to make risotto. Arborio rice, a starchy short-grain variety grown in northern Italy, works well because as the starch cooks, it dissolves and helps form a creamy texture. Look for Arborio rice in a gourmet market.

BUTTERSCOTCH PUDDING

This pudding is lick-the-bowl-clean good. It starts with a simmered egg-and-dairy base, which is mixed with an easy homemade caramel. The pudding is chilled, and topped with a dollop of whipped cream for a home-style treat your friends will appreciate and your mom would be proud of.

1 In a large heatproof bowl, whisk together the egg yolks, cornstarch, and ½ cup (4 fl oz/125 ml) of the milk until well blended. In a small saucepan, combine the remaining 2½ cups (20 fl oz/625 ml) milk, the butter, and a pinch of salt and heat over medium heat, stirring often, until the butter is melted. Set aside and cover to keep warm.

2 In a deep saucepan, combine the sugar and water and stir to moisten the sugar. Place over high heat and bring to a boil, stirring constantly. Stop stirring and cook, brushing down any crystals that form on the inside of the pan with a pastry brush dipped in cold water and occasionally swirling the saucepan by its handle, until the sugar turns a deep golden brown caramel. The caramel will have a toasty aroma, and you may see some wisps of smoke.

3 Reduce the heat to low. Gradually and very carefully stir the warm milk mixture into the caramel; the mixture will boil furiously. Cook, stirring constantly, until the mixture is smooth and the caramel is completely dissolved. Gradually whisk the hot caramel mixture into the egg mixture. Return to the saucepan and heat over medium heat until the mixture comes to a full boil, whisking constantly.

4 Strain the mixture through a sieve placed over another heatproof bowl. Stir in the vanilla extract. Press a piece of plastic wrap directly onto the surface of the pudding, and pierce the plastic a few times with a knife tip to allow the steam to escape. Let cool to lukewarm, then refrigerate until cold, about 2 hours.

5 To serve, divide the pudding among individual bowls and dollop with whipped cream. Serve right away.

Large egg yolks, 6

Cornstarch, ⅓ cup (1½ oz/45 g) plus 1 tablespoon

Whole milk, 3 cups (24 fl oz/750 ml)

Unsalted butter, 6 tablespoons (3 oz/90 g)

Kosher salt

Sugar, 1¼ cups (10 oz/315 g)

Water, ¼ cup (2 fl oz/60 ml)

Pure vanilla extract, 1 teaspoon

Whipped cream, for serving

VANILLA BEAN ICE CREAM

MAKES 1½ QT (1.5 L)

Simmering and freezing aren't often seen together in recipes, but they're essential steps in preparing homemade custard-style ice cream. This version uses whole vanilla beans, which lend their distinctive taste and appealing black flecks to the ice cream. It beats store-bought in texture and flavor any day.

1 In a heavy saucepan, combine the milk, cream, and ¼ cup (2 oz/ 60 g) of the sugar. With the tip of a paring knife, scrape the seeds from the vanilla beans into the pan, then toss the pods into the pan. Place over medium heat and bring just to a simmer, stirring to dissolve the sugar. Remove from the heat and steep for 20 minutes.

2 Meanwhile, in a large heatproof bowl, vigorously whisk together the egg yolks, salt, and the remaining ½ cup (4 oz/125 g) sugar until the mixture falls in a thick, wide ribbon when the whisk is lifted, about 2 minutes.

3 Remove the vanilla bean pods and reheat the milk mixture to a bare simmer. Slowly add the milk mixture to the yolk mixture while whisking constantly. Pour it all back into the saucepan and simmer gently over medium-low heat, stirring often with a wooden spoon, until the mixture is thickened enough to coat the spoon, about 3 minutes. Draw your finger across the spoon. The custard is ready if it does not immediately run back together.

4 Strain the mixture through a fine-mesh sieve into a storage container, let cool to room temperature, and then cover and refrigerate overnight.

5 Pour the cooled mixture into an ice cream maker and freeze according to the manufacturer's directions. You can eat it right out of the machine, if you like, but the texture will be like soft-serve. For a firmer texture and deeper flavor, transfer the ice cream to a tightly covered container and freeze for about 6 hours.

Whole milk, 1½ cups (12 fl oz/375 ml)

Heavy cream, 2½ cups (20 fl oz/625 ml)

Sugar, ¾ cup (6 oz/185 g)

Vanilla beans, 2, split lengthwise

Large egg yolks, 8

Kosher salt, ¼ teaspoon

ALL ABOUT
STEAMING

Steaming is a gentle cooking method that retains the food's shape, color, flavor, and texture. It can be a healthy form of cooking, because there are no oil or added fats involved and the nutrients are retained. During cooking, the rising steam released from a boiling liquid surrounds the food to cook it gently. Some steamed foods, such as shellfish or artichokes, come into direct contact with a small amount of the simmering liquid, but the steam is still the main cooking agent.

Steaming involves gently cooking food while suspended over boiling water in a tightly covered pot. There are many ways to steam, and the method varies slightly with the type of food.

Typically, steaming calls for using a steamer basket, rack, or in the case of Asian-style cooking, a tiered bamboo steamer, all of which help elevate the food above a boiling liquid. Be sure the pot you use has a tight-fitting lid that will accommodate both the food and the rack, as well as hold in the steam as the food is cooking.

Collapsible metal steamer baskets are a versatile option for your kitchen. Because of their folding sides, they can fit in a variety of pots and work with a range of different foods. Look for one with a sturdy construction, perforated holes, 3 or 4 "feet" for stability, and a hook or handle in the center that will help you lift it out of a hot pot. You can also use a metal rack that fits in the pan. A bamboo steamer, thanks to its tiered construction, is a nice option when you are steaming more than one type of food at a time, but it requires a larger, deeper pot in order to work well.

WHY STEAM FOOD?

Steaming is a quicker and gentler cooking method than boiling, so it's a great option for delicate foods. Steaming vegetables also retains more nutrients than boiling them, as some vitamins and other healthful compounds can leach into the cooking liquid. Choose steaming over boiling when it's important to keep the colors of the ingredients vibrant.

WHAT YOU NEED

WIDE SAUCEPAN WITH TIGHT-FITTING LID

SECRETS TO SUCCESS

AVOID CONTACT
When steaming, the food should not come into direct contact with the water. Make sure the steamer basket or insert sits slightly above the water level.

SPREAD EVENLY
Distribute the food in the steamer basket evenly so that the steam can circulate freely around the food. If you don't have a large enough pot, steam the food in batches.

TAKE A PEEK
If ingredients need to steam for a long time, check periodically to make sure the water has not evaporated. Do so quickly, though, so the temperature inside the pot doesn't drop too much.

TAKE GOOD CARE
Hot steam can scald you, so be careful when opening the pot lid. Protect your hand with an oven mitt and open the lid at an angle so that the steam is released away from you.

REMOVE CAREFULLY Take care when retrieving steamed items from the pot after cooking. Collapsible steamer inserts can be unwieldly. Always protect your hands with an oven mitt.

STEAMER BASKET OR BAMBOO STEAMER

PARING KNIFE TO TEST FOR DONENESS

WATER

MEDIUM-HIGH TO HIGH HEAT

HACK A STEAMER

If you don't have a steamer basket or rack that fits inside your cookware, don't despair—it's still possible to steam.

1   Invert a small, short, empty can, such as a clean tuna can, in a saucepan or pot.

2   Place the food to be steamed in a glass baking dish or heatproof plate that is at least an inch smaller in diameter than the pan.

3   Place the dish or plate in the pan so that it sits on the can, suspended over the water. Voila! You have a homemade steamer.

HOW TO
STEAM

1
SET IT UP
Pour water into a deep saucepan.
Add a steamer basket, insert, or rack,
making sure that the water line
is just below the bottom of the rack.

2
ADD THE FOOD
Bring the water to a boil and add
the food to the basket, spreading
it out to distribute it evenly.

3
COVER & STEAM
Cover the pan and let the
food cook in the steam.
Reduce the heat so that the
water simmers and continues
to generate the steam.

4

STEAMING SHELLFISH

Shellfish come with their own
natural "rack" built in. Remove
shellfish from the pot as soon
as their shells open. Leave the others
in the pan to continue steaming.

5

STEAMING FISH

Fish is delicate, so it's best to
steam it in a bamboo steamer
or on a heatproof plate on a rack.

STEAMED ARTICHOKES
WITH GARLIC MAYO

MAKES 4 SERVINGS

This is an easy way to seriously up your crudités-and-dip game. Artichokes and homemade mayo may sound and look fancy, but they're actually easy to prepare. Serve them as an appetizer or first course to impress your friends. You only need about half the mayo, but leftovers are delicious spread inside a crusty bread sandwich.

1 To make the garlic mayo, put the garlic on a cutting board and smash with the flat side of a chef's knife. Pile 1 teaspoon salt on top of the garlic. Using the knife, press and chop the garlic with the salt, working steadily, until it forms a paste. In a large bowl, using an electric mixer, beat the egg yolks until smooth and blended. While whisking, very slowly drizzle in the olive oil, ½ teaspoon at a time, and beat until a thick emulsion forms. After about 2 tablespoons (or 6 additions) of oil have been added, beat in 1 teaspoon oil at a time until all the oil is used. Gently stir in the garlic paste. Season to taste with pepper. Cover and refrigerate until ready to use.

2 Working with 1 artichoke at a time, trim the stem even with the base. Snap off the small tough leaves around the base. Cut off the upper third of the artichoke, then cut each artichoke in half lengthwise. Rub the cut surface of the artichoke with the lemon half to prevent it from turning brown.

3 Select a wide saucepan large enough to hold the artichokes in a single layer. Place a steamer basket or insert in the saucepan and add water to reach the bottom of the basket. Place the artichokes, cut side down, on the rack. Bring the water to a simmer over medium heat. Cover and steam until the base of an artichoke is easily pierced with the tip of a paring knife, about 20 minutes.

4 Transfer the artichokes to individual plates. Sprinkle with flaky sea salt and serve warm or at room temperature, along with the mayo for dipping.

FOR THE GARLIC MAYO
Garlic, 8 cloves

Kosher salt and freshly ground pepper

Large egg yolks, 6, at room temperature

Extra-virgin olive oil, 2 cups (16 fl oz/500 ml)

Globe artichokes, 4

Lemon, ½

Flaky sea salt or kosher salt for sprinkling

MUSSELS
WITH LEMON & ALE

MAKES 4 SERVINGS

Gone are the days when steamed mussels were a summer splurge or happy hour indulgence. This classic bar food can easily be made at home in less than 20 minutes. Toss a few ingredients in the pot, break out an extra ale to sip on while the mussels steam open, and sit back as your kitchen is enveloped in an irresistible aroma.

1 In a large pot over medium heat, melt the butter. Add the shallots and sauté until fragrant, 2–3 minutes. Season with salt and pepper.

2 Raise the heat to high, add the ale and mussels, and toss to combine. Cover and steam, stirring occasionally, until all of the mussels have opened, 3–5 minutes. Using a slotted spoon, transfer the mussels to 4 individual bowls, discarding any that failed to open.

3 Stir the lemon zest and cream into the cooking liquid and simmer until the liquid thickens, about 5 minutes. Ladle the liquid over the mussels, garnish with the parsley, and serve right away with the bread for dipping into the sauce.

{ **PREP WORK: HOW TO DEBEARD MUSSELS**
Some mussels have little fibrous tufts that stick to the outside of the shells. If you see them, they should be removed prior to cooking. Sometimes you can simply pull off the beards, or you may need to use a knife or scissors to separate them. It's best to remove the beards right before cooking.

Unsalted butter, 2 tablespoons

Shallots, 2, minced

Kosher salt and freshly ground pepper

Light Belgian-style ale, 1 cup (8 fl oz/250 ml)

Mussels, 1½ lb (750 g), scrubbed and debearded

Lemon zest, 2 teaspoons grated

Heavy cream, ¼ cup (2 fl oz/60 ml)

Fresh flat-leaf parsley, 1 tablespoon chopped

Crusty bread, for serving

STEAMED HALIBUT
WITH GREEN ONIONS, GINGER & SIZZLING OIL

MAKES 4 SERVINGS

Looking for a light, yet flavorful meal? Want to cook fish without having to worry about how much oil to use? You've come to the right recipe. Here, halibut is steamed along with punchy green onions, then coated in a flavorful Asian sauce. A drizzle of piping hot, onion-infused oil makes an easy finishing sauce.

1 Make a bed of the halved green onions on a heatproof plate large enough to hold the fish, but about 2 inches (5 cm) smaller than the pan you use for steaming. Place the fillets in a single layer on the bed of green onions. Cover and refrigerate until ready to steam.

2 Place a bamboo steamer or steamer rack on the bottom of a wok or large, deep frying pan and pour in water to a depth of 2 inches (5 cm). The water should not touch the steamer. Bring the water to a boil over high heat.

3 Meanwhile, in a bowl, stir together the ginger, garlic, 1 tablespoon of the canola oil, the soy sauce, sesame oil, oyster sauce, sugar, cornstarch, and pepper. Spoon the mixture evenly over the fish fillets.

4 Place the plate on the steamer above the boiling water, cover tightly, and steam until the fish is barely opaque throughout when pierced with the tip of a paring knife, 8–10 minutes. Carefully remove the plate from the steamer and transfer the fillets to a warmed platter. Discard the bed of green onions and spoon any sauce remaining on the plate over the fish.

5 In a small saucepan over high heat, heat the remaining 1 tablespoon canola oil until it is almost smoking. Place the minced green onion on top of the fish. Carefully drizzle the hot oil over the fish and serve right away with the rice.

Green onions, 4, 3 halved crosswise and 1 minced

Halibut fillets, 4, about 6 oz (185 g) each

Fresh ginger, 1 tablespoon, finely chopped

Garlic, 2 cloves, minced

Canola oil, 2 tablespoons

Soy sauce, 1½ tablespoons

Asian sesame oil, 2 teaspoons

Oyster sauce, 1½ teaspoons

Sugar, 1 teaspoon

Cornstarch, 1 teaspoon

Freshly ground pepper, ⅛ teaspoon

Cooked white rice for serving (page 46)

GORGONZOLA-STUFFED RED POTATOES

MAKES 6-8 APPETIZER SERVINGS

This is one of those flavor-packed dishes you'll wish you could eat every day. And amazingly, it works for all three meals: paired with scrambled eggs for brunch, alongside a green salad at lunch, and next to a hunk of roasted meat for dinner. Once you've mastered steaming potatoes, you'll never go back to microwaving them.

1 Pour water into a wide saucepan to a depth of about 1 inch (2.5 cm) and set a steamer basket or insert in the pan. Add water to come just up to the bottom of the steamer and bring to a boil over high heat. When the water comes to a boil, place the potatoes in the steamer, cover, and steam until they are easily pierced with the tip of a paring knife, 20–25 minutes. Using tongs, carefully transfer the potatoes to a cutting board to cool.

2 Using a paring knife, cut a very thin slice off one rounded side of each potato, so it will not roll. Using a small spoon, scoop out a little flesh from the top of the potatoes create a small hollow for the cheese mixture to fit into. Sprinkle the potatoes with salt.

3 In a large bowl, mix the Gorgonzola and cream cheeses together until completely smooth. Add the vinegar, mustard, oil, and lemon juice and stir until well blended. Add the 2 teaspoons chives and the basil and stir to combine. Taste and adjust the seasoning.

4 Generously spoon the filling into the hollow of each potato. Transfer the potatoes to a platter, sprinkle with additional chives, and serve.

Small red potatoes, 24, unpeeled

Kosher salt

Gorgonzola cheese, ⅓ lb (155 g), at room temperature

Cream cheese, ½ lb (250 g), at room temperature

Sherry vinegar, 2 teaspoons

Dijon mustard, 1 teaspoon

Olive oil, 1 teaspoon

Fresh lemon juice, 1 teaspoon

Fresh chives, 2 teaspoons minced, plus more for garnish

Fresh basil, 1 tablespoon chopped

LINGUINE
WITH CLAMS, BACON & TOMATOES

MAKES 4 SERVINGS

A little wine and heat is all it takes to coax open these delicious shellfish, which cook inside their shells, forming a natural steamer. For a rustic presentation, keep the clams in their shells after they've cooked. Serve this dish with a simple green salad for a well-rounded meal.

1 Bring a large pot of salted water to a boil. Add the pasta and simmer, stirring occasionally, until tender but still slightly firm to the bite (aka "al dente"), according to the package directions.

2 Meanwhile, place a large frying pan over medium heat. Add 2 tablespoons of the oil and the bacon and sauté until it is beginning to brown, about 2 minutes. Add the shallot and pepper flakes and sauté for 1 minute. Add the wine and simmer until it is reduced by half, about 1 minute. Add the clams and half of the parsley. Cover the pan and steam until the clams just open, about 4 minutes. Discard any clams that failed to open. Stir in the tomatoes.

3 When the pasta is done, drain the pasta and return it to the pot. Add the remaining 1 tablespoon oil and a generous amount of black pepper and stir to coat. Cover the pot to keep warm.

4 Transfer the pasta to a warmed serving bowl. Pour the sauce and clams over the top, sprinkle with the remaining parsley, and serve right away.

Kosher salt and freshly ground black pepper

Linguine, 1 lb (500 g)

Olive oil, 3 tablespoons

Smoked bacon, 3 oz (90 g) chopped

Shallot, 2 large, thinly sliced

Red pepper flakes, pinch

Dry white wine, 1 cup (8 fl oz/250 ml)

Manila clams, 4 lb (2 kg)

Fresh flat-leaf parsley, ½ cup (⅔ oz/20 g) minced

Cherry tomatoes, 2 cups (12 oz/375 g), halved

{ **WORKING WITH FRESH CLAMS** Buy the freshest clams you can from a fishmonger. Fresh clams should be stored in a shallow bowl, covered in a damp kitchen towel, and refrigerated. Serve them within 2 days of your purchase. Scrub them under running water, with a soft-bristled brush, before cooking. An open or cracked shell is a signal that the clam is no longer alive, and should be discarded.

STEAMED SALMON
WITH CHERMOULA

MAKES 4 SERVINGS

Chermoula is a fancy word for a cilantro- and parsley-based pesto,
Moroccan style. It adds fresh and tangy flavors that steam along with the
salmon. Leftover sauce is delicious mixed with pasta or roasted vegetables.
Serve the salmon with a side of quinoa or roasted potatoes to round out the meal.

1 To make the chermoula, turn on a food processor and drop the garlic cloves, one at a time, through the feed tube to mince them. Stop the machine and add the cilantro, parsley, lemon juice, 1 teaspoon salt, the paprika, cumin, and cayenne and process until blended. Scrape down the sides of the food processor with a rubber spatula. With the machine running, slowly add the oil, processing until smooth and thickened. Measure 3 tablespoons of the chermoula and set aside. Put the remaining chermoula in a serving bowl, cover, and refrigerate.

2 Put the salmon on a platter and rub both sides of the fish with the 3 tablespoons chermoula. Cover with plastic wrap and refrigerate for about 2 hours.

3 Remove the fish and the remaining sauce from the refrigerator and let stand at room temperature for 20 minutes.

4 Pour water into a wide saucepan to a depth of about 1 inch (2.5 cm), and set a steamer rack or inverted can (see note on page 121) in the pan. Bring the water to a simmer over medium-low heat. Arrange the salmon fillets on a heatproof plate, place the plate on the rack, cover the pan tightly, and steam until the fish is firm to the touch and is barely opaque throughout when pierced with the tip of a paring knife, about 8 minutes.

5 Transfer the fish to warmed individual plates and top each fillet with a generous spoonful of the chermoula. Pass the remaining chermoula at the table.

FOR THE CHERMOULA

Garlic, 4 cloves

Fresh cilantro leaves, ⅓ cup (⅓ oz/10 g) firmly packed

Fresh flat-leaf parsley leaves, ⅓ cup (⅓ oz/10 g) firmly packed

Fresh lemon juice, ¼ cup (2 fl oz/60 ml)

Kosher salt

Paprika, 1½ teaspoons

Ground cumin, ¾ teaspoon

Cayenne pepper, ⅛–¼ teaspoon

Olive oil, ½ cup (4 fl oz/125 ml)

Center-cut salmon fillets, 4, about 6 oz (185 g) each, skin removed

SPICY BROCCOLI
WITH GARLIC

MAKES 4-6 SERVINGS

This isn't the wet, tasteless steamed broccoli of your youth. Here, broccoli
is steamed until tender-crisp, then drizzled with a hot garlic-infused oil,
crisp garlic slices, and spicy red pepper flakes. Serve this accompanying your
favorite protein, or stir it into pasta with some grated Parmesan cheese.

1 In a small frying pan over medium-low heat, combine the oil, garlic, and red pepper flakes. Cook, stirring often, until the garlic begins to turn golden, 1–2 minutes. Remove from the heat. Pour the oil through a small fine-mesh sieve set over a heatproof bowl. Reserve the oil and the contents of the sieve separately.

2 Pour water into a wide saucepan to a depth of about 1 inch (2.5 cm) and set a steamer basket or insert in the pan. Add water to come just up to the bottom of the steamer and bring to a boil over high heat. When the water comes to a boil, place the broccoli in the steamer, cover tightly, and steam until tender when pierced with the tip of a paring knife, 4–6 minutes.

3 Transfer the broccoli to a warmed serving dish. Drizzle with the garlic oil and toss to coat. Sprinkle with the crisp garlic slices and red pepper flakes from the sieve and serve right away.

Olive oil, 2 tablespoons

Garlic, 2 cloves, thinly sliced crosswise

Red pepper flakes, ¼ teaspoon

Broccoli, 1 head, (about 1½ lb/750 g), trimmed and cut into 2-inch (5-cm) pieces

CAULIFLOWER
WITH CURRY BUTTER

MAKES 4-6 SERVINGS

Cauliflower can be an intimidating vegetable, but it's actually very versatile to cook and easy to prepare. Just cut off all the stalky green leaves, and chop the white head into similar-sized florets. Here, we mixed up a super-easy curry butter that melts over the just-steamed cauliflower, coating it in deep, creamy flavor.

1 Pour water into a wide saucepan to a depth of about 1 inch (2.5 cm), and set a steamer basket or insert in the pan. Bring the water to a boil over high heat. When the water comes to a boil, place the cauliflower pieces in the steamer, cover tightly, and steam until tender when pierced with the tip of a paring knife, about 5 minutes.

2 In a bowl, stir together the butter, curry powder, lemon zest and juice, salt, sugar, and paprika. Transfer the butter to a serving bowl. Add the hot cauliflower and the parsley to the bowl and toss to coat evenly. Serve right away.

{ INGREDIENT DEMYSTIFIED:
CURRY POWDER   Curry refers to a few things: a stewlike dish flavored with spices, a powdered spice blend, or a paste formed of spices and a little fat. Curry paste typically keeps longer, but the powder is cheaper. Both offer a distinct, bold flavor and most include cumin, curry leaves, cardamom, coriander seeds, fennel seeds, mustard seeds, fenugreek, red and black peppers, and turmeric.

Cauliflower, 1½ lb (750 g), trimmed and cut into 2-inch (5-cm) pieces

Unsalted butter, 4 tablespoons (2 oz/60 g), at room temperature

Curry powder, 2 teaspoons

Lemon zest, 1 teaspoon grated

Fresh lemon juice, 1 teaspoon

Kosher salt, ½ teaspoon

Sugar, ¼ teaspoon

Hot paprika, generous pinch

Fresh flat-leaf parsley, 2 tablespoons chopped

SESAME BOK CHOY

Bok choy has a high water density, so steaming, rather than stir-frying it, preserves some of its structure and crunch. Here, a light dressing of fragrant sesame oil, crunchy sesame seeds, and tender green onions coats the vegetable simply. Adding some sliced mushrooms to the steamer would add nice textural and taste contrast.

1 Pour water into a wide saucepan to a depth of about 1 inch (2.5 cm) and set a steamer basket or insert in the pan. Bring the water to a boil over high heat. When the water comes to a boil, place the bok choy in the steamer, cover tightly, and steam until tender when pierced with the tip of a paring knife, but still slightly crisp at the center, about 4 minutes. Transfer to a serving bowl.

2 Add the green onions, sesame oil, sesame seeds, and a pinch of salt to the bok choy and toss to coat evenly. Serve warm or at room temperature.

Baby bok choy, 4, about ⅓ lb (155 g) each, halved lengthwise

Green onions, 2, thinly sliced

Asian sesame oil, 1½ teaspoons

Sesame seeds, 1 teaspoon

Kosher salt

{ INGREDIENT DEMYSTIFIED: SESAME OIL
There are two varieties of sesame oil: deep amber–colored Asian sesame oil and a pale golden variety. The Asian version is made from pressed sesame seeds, has a strong sesame flavor, and is considered a healthy fat, but it shouldn't be heated, thanks to a low smoke point. The paler oils are less flavorful because they are refined and, thus, have a higher smoke point and can be used for cooking.

STEAMED MAPLE & CRANBERRY BROWN BREAD

MAKES ONE 1½-LB (750-G) LOAF

Steaming breads is an old-school technique, but we like the moist texture and deep flavors it produces. Plus, if your oven is ever out of commission, it's useful to know how to make stove-top bread. In the old days, breads were steamed inside empty coffee cans, but today a cake pan does just as well.

1 Generously butter a 9-inch (23-cm) cake pan. Make sure it will fit easily inside a wide, tall-sided pot with a lid.

2 In a bowl, stir together the cornmeal, whole-wheat flour, rye flour, baking soda, salt, and baking powder. In a small bowl, stir together the buttermilk and maple syrup. Pour into the dry ingredients and beat just until combined. The batter should be slightly lumpy. Stir in the cranberries.

3 Scrape the batter into the prepared pan. Cover tightly with foil. Set the pan on a wire rack in the bottom of a wide, deep pot with a tight-fitting lid, making sure it is centered and level. Add hot water to the pot to come halfway up the sides of the cake pan. Cover the pot and bring the water to a gentle boil. Reduce the heat to a simmer. Steam, checking occasionally to be sure the water has not boiled off and adding more hot water as needed, until the bread is puffed, slightly firm to the touch, and slightly moist, about 1¼ hours. A cake tester inserted into the center should come out clean.

4 Carefully remove the hot pan from the water bath. Transfer to a wire rack and remove the foil. Let stand for a few minutes, then turn the bread out of the pan and let it cool slightly or completely. Cut into wedges to serve.

Butter, for greasing

Stone-ground yellow cornmeal, ¾ cup (3¾ oz/110 g)

Whole-wheat flour, ¾ cup (3¾ oz/110 g)

Rye flour, ¾ cup (2¼ oz/70 g)

Baking soda, 1½ teaspoons

Kosher salt, ¾ teaspoon

Baking powder, ½ teaspoon

Buttermilk, 1½ cups (12 fl oz/375 ml)

Maple syrup, ½ cup (4 fl oz/125 ml)

Dried cranberries, ¾ cup (3 oz/90 g)

Hot water, as needed

INDEX

weldon**owen**

415 Jackson Street, Suite 200, San Francisco, CA 94111
www.weldonowen.com

COOK GOOD FOOD
Conceived and produced by Weldon Owen, Inc.
In collaboration with Williams-Sonoma, Inc.
3250 Van Ness Avenue, San Francisco, CA 94109

A WELDON OWEN PRODUCTION
Copyright © 2014 Weldon Owen, Inc. and Williams-Sonoma, Inc.
All rights reserved, including the right of reproduction
in whole or in part in any form.

Printed and bound in China by 1010 Printing, Ltd.

First printed in 2014
10 9 8 7 6 5 4 3 2 1

Library of Congress Cataloging-in-Publication
data is available

ISBN 13: 978-1-61628-766-5
ISBN 10: 1-61628-766-7

Weldon Owen is a division of
BONNIER

WELDON OWEN, INC.
CEO and President Terry Newell
VP, Sales and Marketing Amy Kaneko
VP, Publisher Roger Shaw

Associate Publisher Jennifer Newens
Assistant Editor Emma Rudolph

Creative Director Kelly Booth
Art Director Ashley Lima
Designer Rachel Lopez Metzger

Production Director Chris Hemesath
Production Manager Michelle Duggan

Photographer Eva Kolenko
Food Stylist Lillian Kang
Prop Stylist Esther Feinman

ACKNOWLEDGMENTS

Weldon Owen wishes to thank the following people for their generous support in producing this book:
Amanda Anselmino, Emma Boys, Jane Tunks Demel, Brian Lackey, and Elizabeth Parson